When we work as a team, we learn new things about our world.

SCHOLASTIC

LITERACY PLACE®

Copyright acknowledgments and credits appear on page 136, which constitutes an extension of this copyright page.

Copyright © 1996 by Scholastic Inc.   All rights reserved.   Printed in the U.S.A.
                                            ISBN 0-590-49104-0
                      7 8 9 10   24   02 01 00

Zoom in

on a Space Center

When we work as a team, we learn new things about our world.

Off to Discovery

Team members share new discoveries.

Daring Destinations

Teams explore to gain knowledge.

WORKSHOP 2

How to Create a Team Profile

84

MEET YOUR CREW

Each crew member aboard the ship is called a specialist. Here's what each specialist does:

ENVIRONMENTAL CONTROL: Keeps air breathable and comfortable; takes care of the fresh water supply.

METEOROLOGIST: Keeps track of weather.

COMMUNICATIONS: Maintains radio

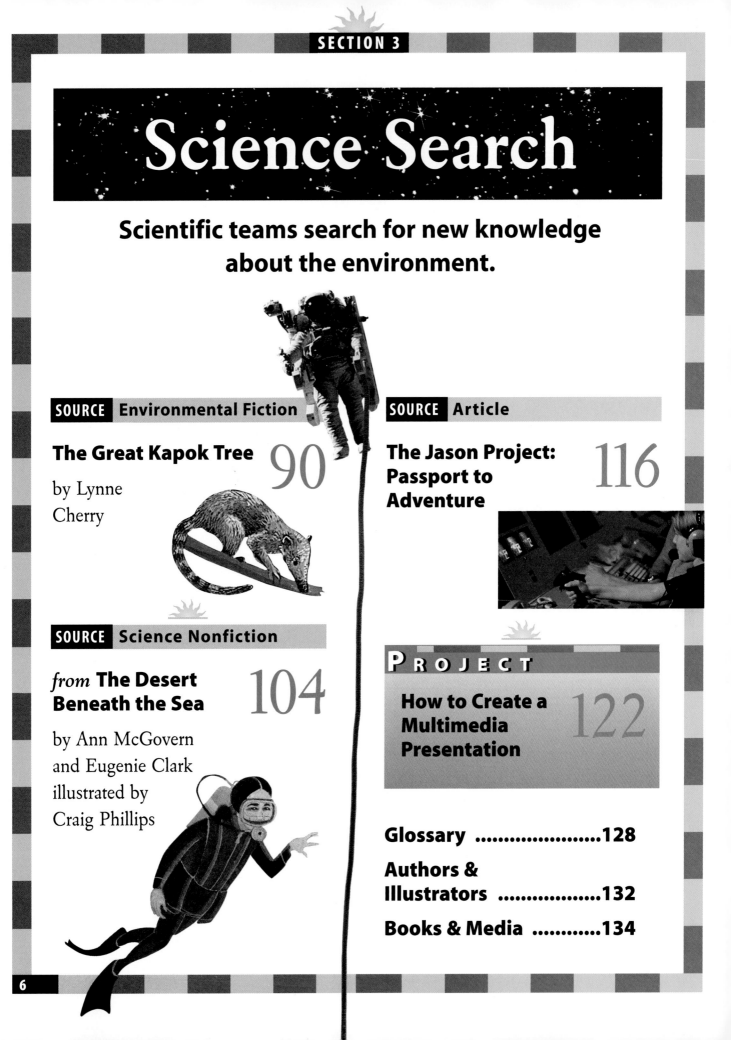

Science Search

Scientific teams search for new knowledge about the environment.

Trade Books

The following books accompany this *Discovery Teams* SourceBook.

Science Nonfiction

AWARD WINNING Author

Digging Up Tyrannosaurus Rex

by John R. Horner and Don Lessem

Fiction

AWARD WINNING Author

Jem's Island

by Kathryn Lasky illustrated by Ronald Himler

Fiction

AWARD WINNING Book

Justin and the Best Biscuits in the World

by Mildred Pitts Walter illustrated by Catherine Stock

Mystery

AWARD WINNING Book

Who Stole The Wizard of Oz?

by Avi illustrated by Derek James

Team members share
new discoveries.

Off to
Discovery

Hike along with a father
and son as they search
for the Lost Lake.
Then go off to
a school that
specializes in
adventure.

Join Sarah and
her new family
as they discover
how a mound of
hay can be as
much fun as a
sand dune.

WORKSHOP 1

Form a team, and make an
exploration map.

THE LOST LAKE

by Allen Say

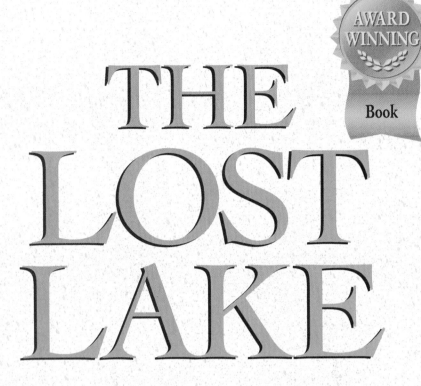

I went to live with Dad last summer.

Every day he worked in his room from morning to night, sometimes on weekends, too. Dad wasn't much of a talker, but when he was busy he didn't talk at all.

I didn't know anybody in the city, so I stayed home most of the time. It was too hot to play outside anyway. In one month I finished all the books I'd brought and grew tired of watching TV.

One morning I started cutting pictures out of old magazines, just to be doing something. They were pictures of mountains and rivers and lakes, and some showed people fishing and canoeing. Looking at them made me feel cool, so I pinned them up in my room.

Dad didn't notice them for two days. When he did, he
looked at them one by one.

"Nice pictures," he said.

"Are you angry with me, Dad?" I asked, because he saved
old magazines for his work.

"It's all right, Luke," he said. "I'm having this place painted
soon anyway."

He thought I was talking about the marks I'd made on
the wall.

That Saturday Dad woke me up early in the morning and
told me we were going camping! I was wide awake in a second.
He gave me a pair of brand-new hiking boots to try out. They
were perfect.

In the hallway I saw a big backpack and a knapsack all
packed and ready to go.

"What's in them, Dad?" I asked.

"Later," he said. "We have a long drive ahead of us."

In the car I didn't ask any more questions because Dad was
so grumpy in the morning.

"Want a sip?" he said, handing me his mug. He'd never let
me drink coffee before. It had lots of sugar in it.

"Where are we going?" I finally asked.

"We're off to the Lost Lake, my lad."

"How can you lose a lake?"

"No one's found it, that's how." Dad was smiling! "Grandpa and I used to go there a long time ago. It was our special place, so don't tell any of your friends."

"I'll never tell," I promised. "How long are we going to stay there?"

"Five days, maybe a week."

"We're going to sleep outside for a whole week?"

"That's the idea."

"Oh, boy!"

We got to the mountains in the afternoon.

"It's a bit of a hike to the lake, son," Dad said.

"I don't mind," I told him. "Are there any fish in the lake?"

"Hope so. We'll have to catch our dinner, you know."

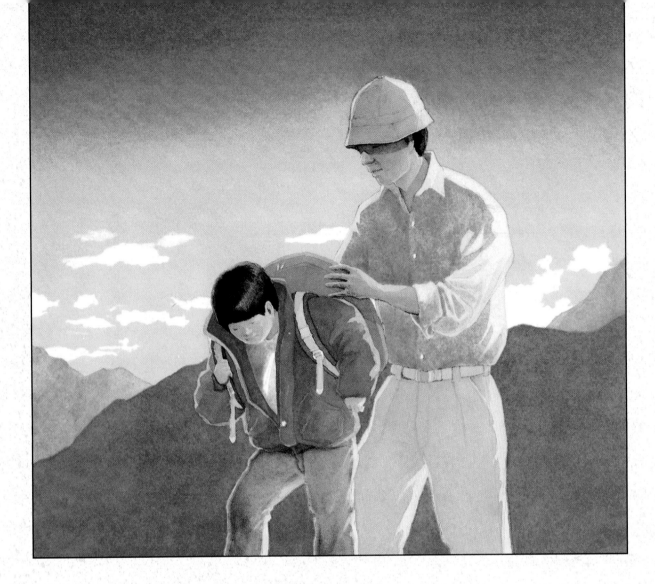

"You didn't bring any food?"

"Of course not. We're going to live like true outdoorsmen."

"Oh . . ."

Dad saw my face and started to laugh. He must have been joking. I didn't think we were going very far anyway, because Dad's pack was so heavy I couldn't even lift it.

Well, Dad was like a mountain goat. He went straight up the trail, whistling all the while. But I was gasping in no time. My knapsack got very heavy and I started to fall behind.

Dad stopped for me often, but he wouldn't let me take off my pack. If I did I'd be too tired to go on, he said.

It was almost suppertime when we got to the lake.

The place reminded me of the park near Dad's apartment.
He wasn't whistling or humming anymore.

"Welcome to the *Found* Lake," he muttered from the side
of his mouth.

"What's wrong, Dad?"

"Do you want to camp with all these people around us?"

"I don't mind."

"Well, I do!"

"Are we going home?"

"Of course not!"

He didn't even take off his pack. He just turned and started to walk away.

Soon the lake was far out of sight.

Then it started to rain. Dad gave me a poncho and it kept me dry, but I wondered where we were going to sleep that night. I wondered what we were going to do for dinner. I wasn't sure about camping anymore.

I was glad when Dad finally stopped and set up the tent. The rain and wind beat against it, but we were warm and cozy inside. And Dad had brought food. For dinner we had salami and dried apricots.

"I'm sorry about the lake, Dad," I said.

He shook his head. "You know something, Luke? There aren't any secret places left in the world anymore."

"What if we go very far up in the mountains? Maybe we can find our own lake."

"There are lots of lakes up here, but that one was special."

"But we've got a whole week, Dad."

"Well, why not? Maybe we'll find a lake that's not on the map."

"Sure, we will!"

We started early in the morning. When the fog cleared we saw other hikers ahead of us. Sure enough, Dad became very glum.

"We're going cross-country, partner," he said.

"Won't we get lost?"

"A wise man never leaves home without his compass."

So we went off the trail. The hills went on and on. The mountains went on and on. It was kind of lonesome. It seemed as if Dad and I were the only people left in the world.

And then we hiked into a big forest.

At noontime we stopped by a creek and ate lunch and drank ice-cold water straight from the stream. I threw rocks in the water, and fish, like shadows, darted in the pools.

"Isn't this a good place to camp, Dad?"

"I thought we were looking for our lake."

"Yes, right . . ." I mumbled.

The forest went on and on.

"I don't mean to scare you, son," Dad said. "But we're in bear country. We don't want to surprise them, so we have to make a lot of noise. If they hear us, they'll just go away."

What a time to tell me! I started to shout as loudly as I could. Even Dad wouldn't be able to beat off bears. I thought about those people having fun back at the lake. I thought about the creek, too, with all those fish in it. That would have been a fine place to camp. The Lost Lake hadn't been so bad either.

It was dark when we got out of the forest. We built a fire
and that made me feel better. Wild animals wouldn't come near
a fire. Dad cooked beef stroganoff and it was delicious.

Later it was bedtime. The sleeping bag felt wonderful. Dad
and I started to count the shooting stars, then I worried that
maybe we weren't going to find our lake.

"What are you thinking about, Luke?" Dad asked.

"I didn't know you could cook like that," I said.

Dad laughed. "That was only freeze-dried stuff. When we
get home, I'll cook you something really special."

"You know something, Dad? You seem like a different person up here."

"Better or worse?"

"A lot better."

"How so?"

"You talk more."

"I'll have to talk more often, then."

That made me smile. Then I slept.

Dad shook me awake. The sun was just coming up, turning everything all gold and orange and yellow. And there was the lake, right in front of us.

For a long time we watched the light change on the water, getting brighter and brighter. Dad didn't say a word the whole time. But then, I didn't have anything to say either.

After breakfast we climbed a mountain and saw our lake below us. There wasn't a sign of people anywhere. It really seemed as if Dad and I were all alone in the world.

I liked it just fine.

SOURCE

NATIONAL GEOGRAPHIC
world

Magazine

AWARD
WINNING

Magazine

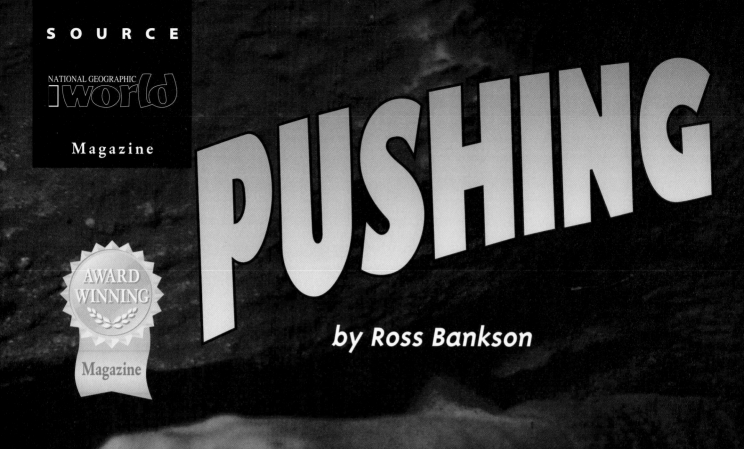

PUSHING

by Ross Bankson

Finally, it's summertime! The season to kick back, relax, and get set for—school? Why not? It just depends on your idea of school. Adventure Quest is a school for the *outdoors*. "We teach recreation skills you can use for the rest of your life," says the director, Peter Kennedy. You'll find week-long courses in white-water and wilderness canoeing, kayaking, rock climbing, caving, backpacking, and mountain biking.

THE LIMITS

▲ *The dark, mysterious world of a cave in Vermont awaits discovery by Pierre Harrison-Beauregard, 13, of New Bedford, Massachusetts. Squeezing through the cave's tight spaces was exciting— "but a little scary too," he says.*

◄ **SCALING
A ROCK FACE**
*Chris Hackett, 10, of
Manhasset, New York,
looks below. "With
the harness and ropes,
you couldn't fall,"
he says.*

Climbing Lingo

BELAYER (bih-LAY-er) *person
who controls the rope attached
to the climber*

CARABINER (kair-uh-BEE-ner)
*oblong metal ring used to hold
a freely running rope*

▲ **ON THE ROPES**
*A climber meets a steep challenge.
He is secured by a rope that runs up, through
a carabiner anchored to a tree, then down to the
belayer on the ground.*

▲ **WE DID IT!** *Students celebrate victory atop a conquered cliff. A ropes course and a practice wall helped prepare them for the real thing.*

Younger students can choose a sampler that has two sports. "I love climbing jungle gyms, trees, anything—so I knew I'd like rock climbing best," says 9-year-old Paul Cancro, of Wall Township, New Jersey. "But I learned other things too, like how to escape from a kayak underwater and how to steer a canoe."

The base camp for Adventure Quest is in Woodstock, Vermont, but students may go biking along steep country roads in New Hampshire or caving in New York State. Advanced students may climb the Rocky Mountains or kayak angry rapids in Canada.

▲ **A SUCCESSFUL ROLL** *brings a smile to Jacey Cobb, right, and praise from her instructor. "Rolling over in a kayak was great—once you learned how," says Jacey.*

"We had a totally wild adventure canoeing in white water," says Luke Moore, 13, of North Pomfret, Vermont. "Where the water backwashes, you have to lean the right way or else you'll tip over."

Luke and his brother, Brendan, didn't tackle white water before they were ready, though. With one instructor for every three students, training is safe but demanding. "We stress the three S's: supervision, skills, and safety," says Kennedy. And the training pays off, according to the students. Says Jacey Cobb, 11, of Norwich, Vermont, who took kayaking at Adventure Quest: "I never dreamed I could do the things I did."

White-water rating scale

I *Very easy.*

II *Easy. Moderate rapids.*

III *Medium difficulty. Lots of waves.*

IV *Expert. Long, violent, irregular waves up to 5 feet.*

V *Almost continuous violent rapids, waves over 5 feet. Dangerous rocks, holes, lots of turns.*

VI *Extremely dangerous.*

▲ **CLASS III RAPIDS**—*That's what this team braved on the Connecticut River. "Running the rapids was wet, but awesome," says Brendan Moore, 11, in front. He and his brother Luke, in back, rank among the top junior canoeing teams in the United States.*

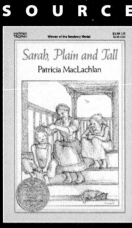

from

Sarah, Plain and Tall

by Patricia MacLachlan
illustrated by Marni Backer

Caleb and Anna Witting live with their father on the prairie. Their mother died when Caleb was a baby, leaving them with memories of a mother who sang while she worked. Anna, Caleb, and their father are lonely. One day Mr. Witting advertises in a newspaper for a wife. He receives an answer from Sarah Wheaton, who lives by the ocean in Maine with her brother, William. After several letters back and forth, Sarah decides to visit the family for a month. She writes that she is "plain and tall" and that she likes to sing. Caleb and Anna are excited to meet Sarah and her cat Seal.

Sarah came in the spring. She came through green grass fields that bloomed with Indian paintbrush, red and orange, and blue-eyed grass.

Papa got up early for the long day's trip to the train and back. He brushed his hair so slick and shiny that Caleb laughed. He wore a clean blue shirt, and a belt instead of suspenders.

He fed and watered the horses, talking to them as he hitched them up to the wagon. Old Bess, calm and kind; Jack, wild-eyed, reaching over to nip Bess on the neck.

"Clear day, Bess," said Papa, rubbing her nose.

"Settle down, Jack." He leaned his head on Jack.

And then Papa drove off along the dirt road to fetch Sarah. Papa's new wife. Maybe. Maybe our new mother.

Gophers ran back and forth across the road, stopping to stand up and watch the wagon. Far off in the field a woodchuck ate and listened. Ate and listened.

Caleb and I did our chores without talking. We shoveled out the stalls and laid down new hay. We fed the sheep. We swept and straightened and carried wood and water. And then our chores were done.

Caleb pulled on my shirt.

"Is my face clean?" he asked. "Can my face be *too* clean?" He looked alarmed.

"No, your face is clean but not too clean," I said.

Caleb slipped his hand into mine as we stood on the porch, watching the road. He was afraid.

"Will she be nice?" he asked. "Like Maggie?"

"Sarah will be nice," I told him.

"How far away is Maine?" he asked.

"You know how far. Far away, by the sea."

"Will Sarah bring some sea?" he asked.

"No, you cannot bring the sea."

The sheep ran in the field, and far off the cows moved slowly to the pond, like turtles.

"Will she like us?" asked Caleb very softly.

I watched a marsh hawk wheel down behind the barn.

He looked up at me.

"Of course she will like us." He answered his own question. "We are nice," he added, making me smile.

We waited and watched. I rocked on the porch and Caleb rolled a marble on the wood floor. Back and forth. Back and forth. The marble was blue.

We saw the dust from the wagon first, rising above the road, above the heads of Jack and Old Bess. Caleb climbed up onto the porch roof and shaded his eyes.

"A bonnet!" he cried. "I see a yellow bonnet!"

The dogs came out from under the porch, ears up, their eyes on the cloud of dust bringing Sarah. The wagon passed the fenced field, and the cows and sheep looked up, too. It rounded the windmill and the barn and the windbreak of Russian olive that Mama had planted long ago. Nick began to bark, then Lottie, and the wagon clattered into the yard and stopped by the steps.

"Hush," said Papa to the dogs.

And it was quiet.

Sarah stepped down from the wagon, a cloth bag in her hand. She reached up and took off her yellow bonnet, smoothing back her brown hair into a bun. She was plain and tall.

"Did you bring some sea?" cried Caleb beside me.

"Something from the sea," said Sarah, smiling. "And me." She turned and lifted a black case from the wagon. "And Seal, too."

Carefully she opened the case, and Seal, gray with white feet, stepped out. Lottie lay down, her head on her paws, staring. Nick leaned down to sniff. Then he lay down, too.

"The cat will be good in the barn," said Papa. "For mice."

Sarah smiled. "She will be good in the house, too."

Sarah took Caleb's hand, then mine. Her hands were large and rough. She gave Caleb a shell—a moon snail, she called it—that was curled and smelled of salt.

"The gulls fly high and drop the shells on the rocks below," she told Caleb. "When the shell is broken, they eat what is inside."

"That is very smart," said Caleb.

"For you, Anna," said Sarah, "a sea stone."

And she gave me the smoothest and whitest stone I had ever seen.

"The sea washes over and over and around the stone, rolling it until it is round and perfect."

"That is very smart, too," said Caleb. He looked up at Sarah. "We do not have the sea here."

Sarah turned and looked out over the plains.

"No," she said. "There is no sea here. But the land rolls a little like the sea."

My father did not see her look, but I did. And I knew that Caleb had seen it, too. Sarah was not smiling. Sarah was already lonely. In a month's time the preacher might come to marry Sarah and Papa. And a month was a long time. Time enough for her to change her mind and leave us.

Papa took Sarah's bags inside, where her room was ready with a quilt on the bed and blue flax dried in a vase on the night table.

Seal stretched and made a small cat sound. I watched her circle the dogs and sniff the air. Caleb came out and stood beside me.

"When will we sing?" he whispered.

I shook my head, turning the white stone over and over in my hand. I wished everything was as perfect as the stone. I wished that Papa and Caleb and I were perfect for Sarah. I wished we had a sea of our own.

The dogs loved Sarah first. Lottie slept beside her bed, curled in a soft circle, and Nick leaned his face on the covers in the morning, watching for the first sign that Sarah was awake. No one knew where Seal slept. Seal was a roamer.

Sarah's collection of shells sat on the windowsill.

"A scallop," she told us, picking up the shells one by one, "a sea clam, an oyster, a razor clam. And a conch shell. If you put it to your ear you can hear the sea." She put it to Caleb's ear, then mine. Papa listened, too. Then Sarah listened once more, with a look so sad and far away that Caleb leaned against me.

"At least Sarah can hear the sea," he whispered.

Papa was quiet and shy with Sarah, and so was I. But Caleb talked to Sarah from morning until the light left the sky.

"Where are you going?" he asked. "To do what?"

"To pick flowers," said Sarah. "I'll hang some of them upside down and dry them so they'll keep some color. And we can have flowers all winter long."

"I'll come, too!" cried Caleb. "Sarah said winter," he said to me. "That means Sarah will stay."

Together we picked flowers, paintbrush and clover and prairie violets. There were buds on the wild roses that climbed up the paddock fence.

"The roses will bloom in early summer," I told Sarah. I looked to see if she knew what I was thinking. Summer was when the wedding would be. *Might* be. Sarah and Papa's wedding.

We hung the flowers from the ceiling in little bunches. "I've never seen this before," said Sarah. "What is it called?"

"Bride's bonnet," I told her.

Caleb smiled at the name.

"We don't have this by the sea," she said. "We have seaside goldenrod and wild asters and woolly ragwort."

"Woolly ragwort!" Caleb whooped. He made up a song.

> *"Woolly ragwort all around,*
> *Woolly ragwort on the ground.*
> *Woolly ragwort grows and grows,*
> *Woolly ragwort in your nose."*

Sarah and Papa laughed, and the dogs lifted their heads and thumped their tails against the wood floor. Seal sat on a kitchen chair and watched us with yellow eyes.

We ate Sarah's stew, the late light coming through the windows. Papa had baked bread that was still warm from the fire.

"The stew is fine," said Papa.

"Ayuh." Sarah nodded. "The bread, too."

"What does 'ayuh' mean?" asked Caleb.

"In Maine it means yes," said Sarah. "Do you want more stew?"

"Ayuh," said Caleb.

"Ayuh," echoed my father.

After dinner Sarah told us about William. "He has a gray-and-white boat named *Kittiwake*." She looked out the window. "That is a small gull found way off the shore where William fishes. There are three aunts who live near us. They wear silk dresses and no shoes. You would love them."

"Ayuh," said Caleb.

"Does your brother look like you?" I asked.

"Yes," said Sarah. "He is plain and tall."

At dusk Sarah cut Caleb's hair on the front steps, gathering his curls and scattering them on the fence and ground. Seal batted some hair around the porch as the dogs watched.

"Why?" asked Caleb.

"For the birds," said Sarah. "They will use it for their nests. Later we can look for nests of curls."

"Sarah said 'later,'" Caleb whispered to me as we spread his hair about. "Sarah will stay."

Sarah cut Papa's hair, too. No one else saw, but I found him behind the barn, tossing the pieces of hair into the wind for the birds.

Sarah brushed my hair and tied it up in back with a rose velvet ribbon she had brought from Maine. She brushed hers long and free and tied it back, too, and we stood side by side looking into the mirror. I looked taller, like Sarah, and fair and thin. And with my hair pulled back I looked a little like her daughter. Sarah's daughter.

And then it was time for singing.

Sarah sang us a song we had never heard before as we sat on the porch, insects buzzing in the dark, the rustle of cows in the grasses. It was called "Sumer Is Icumen in," and she taught it to us all, even Papa, who sang as if he had never stopped singing.

> *"Sumer is icumen in,*
> *Lhude sing cuccu!"*

"What is sumer?" asked Caleb. He said it "soomer," the way Sarah had said it.

"Summer," said Papa and Sarah at the same time. Caleb and I looked at each other. Summer was coming.

"Tomorrow," said Sarah, "I want to see the sheep. You know, I've never touched one."

"Never?" Caleb sat up.

"Never," said Sarah. She smiled and leaned back in her chair. "But I've touched seals. Real seals. They are cool and slippery and they slide through the water like fish. They can cry and sing. And sometimes they bark, a little like dogs."

Sarah barked like a seal. And Lottie and Nick came running from the barn to jump up on Sarah and lick her face and make her laugh. Sarah stroked them and scratched their ears and it was quiet again.

"I wish I could touch a seal right now," said Caleb, his voice soft in the night.

"So do I," said Sarah. She sighed, then she began to sing the summer song again. Far off in a field, a meadowlark sang, too.

The sheep made Sarah smile. She sank her fingers into their thick, coarse wool. She talked to them, running with the lambs, letting them suck on her fingers. She named them after her favorite aunts, Harriet and Mattie and Lou. She lay down in the field beside them and sang, "Sumer Is Icumen in," her voice drifting over the meadow grasses, carried by the wind.

She cried when we found a lamb that had died, and she shouted and shook her fist at the turkey buzzards that came from nowhere to eat it. She would not let Caleb or me come near. And that night, Papa went with a shovel to bury the sheep and a lantern to bring Sarah back. She sat on the porch alone. Nick crept up to lean against her knees.

After dinner, Sarah drew pictures to send home to Maine. She began a charcoal drawing of the fields, rolling like the sea rolled. She drew a sheep whose ears were too big. And she drew a windmill.

"Windmill was my first word," said Caleb. "Papa told me so."

"Mine was flower," I said. "What was yours, Sarah?"

"Dune," said Sarah.

"Dune?" Caleb looked up.

"In Maine," said Sarah, "there are rock cliffs that rise up at the edge of the sea. And there are hills covered with pine and spruce trees, green with needles. But William and I found a sand dune all our own. It was soft and sparkling with bits of mica, and when we were little we would slide down the dune into the water."

Caleb looked out the window.

"We have no dunes here," he said.

Papa stood up.

"Yes we do," he said. He took the lantern and went out the door to the barn.

"We do?" Caleb called after him.

He ran ahead, Sarah and I following, the dogs close behind.

Next to the barn was Papa's mound of hay for bedding, nearly half as tall as the barn, covered with canvas to keep the rain from rotting it. Papa carried the wooden ladder from the barn and leaned it against the hay.

"There." He smiled at Sarah. "Our dune."

Sarah was very quiet. The dogs looked up at her, waiting. Seal brushed against her legs, her tail in the air. Caleb reached over and took her hand.

"It looks high up," he said. "Are you scared, Sarah?"

"Scared? Scared!" exclaimed Sarah. "You bet I'm not scared."

She climbed the ladder, and Nick began to bark. She climbed to the very top of the hay and sat, looking down at us. Above, the stars were coming out. Papa piled a bed of loose hay below with his pitchfork. The light of the lantern made his eyes shine when he smiled up at Sarah.

"Fine?" called Papa.

"Fine," said Sarah. She lifted her arms over her head and slid down, down, into the soft hay. She lay, laughing, as the dogs rolled beside her.

"Was it a good dune?" called Caleb.

"Yes," said Sarah. "It is a fine dune."

Caleb and I climbed up and slid down. And Sarah did it three more times. At last Papa slid down, too, as the sky grew darker and the stars blinked like fireflies. We were covered with hay and dust, and we sneezed.

In the kitchen, Caleb and I washed in the big wooden tub and Sarah drew more pictures to send to William. One was of Papa, his hair curly and full of hay. She drew Caleb, sliding down the hay, his arms like Sarah's over his head.

And she drew a picture of me in the tub, my hair long and straight and wet. She looked at her drawing of the fields for a long time.

"Something is missing," she told Caleb. "Something." And she put it away.

"'Dear William,'" Sarah read to us by lantern light that night. "'Sliding down our dune of hay is almost as fine as sliding down the sand dunes into the sea.'"

Caleb smiled at me across the table. He said nothing, but his mouth formed the words I had heard, too. *Our dune.*

The days grew longer. The cows moved close to the pond, where the water was cool and there were trees.

Papa taught Sarah how to plow the fields, guiding the plow behind Jack and Old Bess, the reins around her neck. When the chores were done we sat in the meadow with the sheep, Sarah beside us, watching Papa finish.

"Tell me about winter," said Sarah.

Old Bess nodded her head as she walked, but we could hear Papa speak sharply to Jack.

"Jack doesn't like work," said Caleb. "He wants to be here in the sweet grass with us."

"I don't blame him," said Sarah. She lay back in the grass with her arms under her head. "Tell me about winter," she said again.

"Winter is cold here," said Caleb, and Sarah and I laughed.

"Winter is cold everywhere," I said.

"We go to school in winter," said Caleb. "Sums and writing and books," he sang.

"I am good at sums and writing," said Sarah. "I love books. How do you get to school?"

"Papa drives us in the wagon. Or we walk the three miles when there is not too much snow."

Sarah sat up. "Do you have lots of snow?"

"Lots and lots and lots of snow," chanted Caleb, rolling around in the grass. "Sometimes we have to dig our way out to feed the animals."

"In Maine the barns are attached to the houses sometimes," said Sarah.

Caleb grinned. "So you could have a cow to Sunday supper?"

Sarah and I laughed.

"When there are bad storms, Papa ties a rope from the house to the barn so no one will get lost," said Caleb.

I frowned. I loved winter.

"There is ice on the windows on winter mornings," I told Sarah. "We can draw sparkling pictures and we can see our breath in the air. Papa builds a warm fire, and we bake hot biscuits and put on hundreds of sweaters. And if the snow is too high, we stay home from school and make snow people."

Sarah lay back in the tall grasses again, her face nearly hidden.

"And is there wind?" she asked.

"Do you like wind?" asked Caleb.

"There is wind by the sea," said Sarah.

"There is wind here," said Caleb happily. "It blows the snow and brings tumbleweeds and makes the sheep run. Wind and wind and wind!" Caleb stood up and ran like the wind, and the sheep ran after him. Sarah and I watched him jump over rock and gullies, the sheep behind him, stiff legged and fast. He circled the field, the sun making the top of his hair golden. He collapsed next to Sarah, and the lambs pushed their wet noses into us.

"Hello, Lou," said Sarah, smiling. "Hello, Mattie."

The sun rose higher, and Papa stopped to take off his hat and wipe his face with his sleeve.

"I'm hot," said Sarah. "I can't wait for winter wind. Let's swim."

"Swim where?" I asked her.

"I can't swim," said Caleb.

"Can't swim!" exclaimed Sarah. "I'll teach you in the cow pond."

"That's for cows!" I cried.

But Sarah had grabbed our hands and we were running through the fields, ducking under the fence to the far pond.

"Shoo, cows," said Sarah as the cows looked up, startled. She took off her dress and waded into the water in her petticoat. She dived suddenly and disappeared for a moment as Caleb and I watched. She came up, laughing, her hair streaming free. Water beads sat on her shoulders.

She tried to teach us how to float. I sank like a bucket filled with water and came up sputtering. But Caleb lay on his back and learned how to blow streams of water high in the air like a whale. The cows stood on the banks of the pond and stared and stopped their chewing. Water bugs circled us.

"Is this like the sea?" asked Caleb.

Sarah treaded water.

"The sea is salt," said Sarah. "It stretches out as far as you can see. It gleams like the sun on glass. There are waves."

"Like this?" asked Caleb, and he pushed a wave at Sarah, making her cough and laugh.

"Yes," she said. "Like that."

I held my breath and floated at last, looking up into the sky, afraid to speak. Crows flew over, three in a row. And I could hear a killdeer in the field.

We climbed the bank and dried ourselves and lay in the grass again. The cows watched, their eyes sad in their dinner-plate faces. And I slept, dreaming a perfect dream. The fields had turned to a sea that gleamed like sun on glass. And Sarah was happy.

How to
Make an Exploration Map

When explorers travel to far-off places, they are finding new routes and discovering geographical features that may not have been recorded before. Explorers often mark their routes on special exploration maps.

What is an exploration map? An exploration map shows an explorer's route through a certain area. It also includes the usual information shown on a map: natural features such as mountains, volcanoes, and rivers; and features created by people, such as roads and borders.

N
W E
S

0 200 400 600 m

ASIA

Mongolia

Gobi Desert

China

Loyang

(Persia)

Hormuz

Himalayas

Tibet

Yangtze

Ganges

Chittagong

India

Calicut

Maldive Islands

INDIAN OCEAN

KEY TO MAP
- - - Main Silk Route
— — — Main Spice Route
——— Cheng Ho

SOUTH CHINA SEA

Sumatra

Borneo

Java

Many maps use symbols such as arrows and colored lines to stand for different routes.

Important places like oceans and mountains are included on the map.

The map legend tells what the symbols on the map represent.

The green line shows the routes traveled by the explorer Cheng Ho.

1 Brainstorm a Common Goal

Break into teams and brainstorm a list of ideas for your map. Think of interesting places you've been, places you've learned about through books or movies, or local places of interest. Each team member should make a suggestion. Take a team vote to find out which is the most popular idea.

TOOLS

- paper and pencil
- colored markers
- tracing paper
- ruler
- reference books and maps

2 Research Your Place

- Find maps or pictures of the place that your team selected. As a group, study the maps or pictures and decide what parts you want to include.

- Draw the outline of the map. Then sketch in some of the important features.

- Each team member can draw his or her own route on the map. Have each person use a different color.

- Add landmarks to help guide you on your way.

3 Create Map Symbols

With your group, create symbols that will show important features on your map. For example, you may wish to use blue lines for rivers and dotted lines for borders. Make the symbols look like the things they represent, such as trees to show a forest or ships to show a harbor. Add these symbols to your map's legend. A map legend is a list of the symbols that appear on the map. Next to each symbol is an explanation of what it stands for.

Tips
- Choose a place you all want to learn more about.
- Sketch the map in pencil first, in case you need to make changes.
- Research the place you want to make a map of. You never know what interesting facts you'll discover.

4 Finish and Display Your Map

When your team is satisfied with the map, use colored markers to draw the final outline, features, and routes. Working with your team, display the map. Explain to the class why you selected your route and what they would see if they took that route.

If You Are Using a Computer ...

Create your map on the computer, using the Paint Tools. Use clip art, such as arrows, to create the symbols for your map.

THINK

Why is it important to bring maps on an expedition?

Dr. Mae Jemison
Astronaut ▶

Daring Destinations

Follow Matthew Henson and Robert Peary to the North Pole. Then read about a group of kids who travel to Antarctica.

Meet former astronaut Dr. Mae Jemison.

Take a trip into the future and find out what it's like to visit Earth for the first time.

WORKSHOP 2

Decide on a place you want to explore, and then make a team profile.

MEET YOUR CREW

Each crew member aboard the ship is called a specialist. Here's what each specialist does:

ENVIRONMENTAL CONTROL:
Keeps air breathable and comfortable; takes care of the fresh water supply.

METEOROLOGIST:
Keeps track of weather.

COMMUNICATIONS:
radio contact between
command

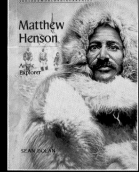
PEARY & HENSON

ATLA

54

All the Way There

by
Sean Dolan

*B*y the end of the 1800s, many people had tried to reach the North Pole but failed. The most famous attempt, made by Adolphus Greeley's team, came the closest. Commander Robert Peary and his aide Matthew Henson had also led many unsuccessful expeditions. Against all odds, they continued their effort to reach their goal—the top of the world.

Henson relaxes on top of one of the sleds he built for travel in the Arctic. In addition to his carpentry skills, Henson was an expert handler of a dog team.

Henson and Peary returned to the Arctic four times between 1896 and 1908, but they could not reach the North Pole. The first two trips, made in 1896 and 1897, were the most successful. Using the *Hope* and a gigantic crane, Peary and Henson managed to remove a huge meteorite, weighing 35 tons, that had fallen on Greenland long ago. (A meteorite is a large particle of matter, similar to rock or stone, from outer space.) The meteorite immediately went on display in the Museum of Natural History in New York City. It added to Peary's fame, but it did not make him feel any better about his failure to reach the North Pole.

The most frustrating trip began in 1898. Peary now had a new plan. Using a specially designed ship called the *Windward,*

Peary planned to sail much farther northward along Greenland's coast before landing. This way, his party would not have to travel so far over land to reach the Pole. The *Windward* was supposed to have engines so powerful that it could batter its way through the Arctic ice.

The plan did not work. In the fall of 1898, the ship became hopelessly stuck in ice off Ellesmere Island, which is just to the west of Greenland. Peary announced a new scheme. The men would abandon the *Windward* and march to Fort Conger. The fort was on the northern shore of Ellesmere Island. It was also the place where the men of the Greeley expedition had waited in vain to be rescued.

In temperatures of 60 degrees below zero, Henson cut a trail through the ice to Fort Conger. Although it was already winter, Peary insisted on starting out immediately. It was a bad mistake. This was a different sort of journey than any he and Henson had taken before. Beneath the ice this time was not land, as on Greenland, but the waters of the Arctic Ocean. At different spots huge and strangely shaped pressure ridges sprang up. These were created by the force of two bodies of ice crashing into each other, driven by the ocean currents beneath them. At night, Peary, Henson, and the four Eskimos who traveled with them could hear the ice groaning and creaking. Sometimes the explorers came upon huge open areas of water where the ice had opened up. They would then have to change direction to get around them.

Peary and Henson made it to Fort Conger, but at great cost. Peary's feet became badly frostbitten, and he was unable to walk. Henson strapped him to his sled and in only 11 days brought him the 250 miles back to the *Windward,* where the ship's doctor was forced to cut off all but the big toe on each of Peary's feet.

Several dog teams and sleds travel across the Arctic ice. Notice how the dogs fan out to pull their loads rather than work side by side in pairs of two along a tight column. This makes pulling easier, but it is possible only in landscapes where there are no trees or other obstacles.

Despite this setback, Peary was determined to stay in the Arctic. He and Henson remained for four more years. During that time, they made three separate attempts at the Pole. All fell short. On April 21, 1902, Peary wrote in his journal, "The game is off. My dream of 16 years is ended. . . . I cannot accomplish the impossible." The discouraged explorers returned home.

Henson also thought that the quest had come to an end. Even before the last expedition, he had begun to tell friends that he was through with Arctic exploration, but his friend George Gardner had convinced him to continue by telling him how important it was for black Americans to have Henson as a role model. Blacks are proud of you and all that you have achieved, Gardner told his friend. Think how proud they will be if a black man reaches the North Pole. Still, Henson was glad to have a break from his polar labors. After he returned to the United States, he took a job on the Pennsylvania Railroad, which enabled him to see much of the country. He also asked his sweetheart, Lucy Ross, to marry him.

ATLA

But Peary could not abandon his dream forever, and neither could Henson. In 1905, Peary set off on a new expedition, and Henson was with him. This time, a new ship, the *Roosevelt,* succeeded in smashing its way through the Arctic ice. Sledding over extremely treacherous ice, Henson and Peary came within 175 miles of the Pole. This was the closest that anyone had ever come. They returned to the United States both frustrated and certain that next time they would make it.

Peary and Henson's sixth polar expedition departed from Long Island, New York, on July 6, 1908. With the two men this time were four other adventurers. All of them were younger than the 42-year-old Henson, but Henson knew that his vast experience would more than make up for the youthful high spirits of his comrades.

This time the expedition had good luck right from the beginning. The weather was just cold enough to keep the surface frozen with a minimum of breaks in the ice, but not too cold to work and travel in. Henson wrote in his diary that he had never seen such smooth sea ice, and the group made rapid progress. After every five days, Peary sent one of the members of his party back to the ship. The final assault on the Pole would be made by just Peary, one other member of his expedition, and a couple of Eskimos. In this way, only a small load of supplies would have to be carried the entire length of the journey. But who Peary would ask to join him at the Pole remained a mystery.

The explorers continued on, averaging a very fast 16 miles a day. On March 28, 1909, they passed the farthest point north they had ever reached. Two days later, Peary asked the third remaining member of the expedition to return to the ship. Matthew Henson would go with him to the North Pole.

The next day, April 1, Peary, Henson, and four Eskimos, Seegloo, Ootah, Eginwah, and Ooqueah, began their final dash for the Pole, which was now 130 miles away. Because of his crippled feet Peary was traveling slowly, but Henson drove his lead team at a furious pace. On the morning of April 6, Henson woke up Seegloo and Ootah. "Ahdoolo! . . . Ahdoolo!" he called, a little more urgently than usual. They were just 35 miles from the Pole.

At Peary's orders, Henson and the two Eskimos forged ahead. They were supposed to stop just short of the Pole to let Peary catch up. That afternoon, when Henson stopped for a rest, he realized that he had made a mistake. If his calculation was correct, he had not only reached the Pole, but gone beyond it! He backtracked a little bit and waited for Peary. The commander of the expedition took out his instruments, took his readings, and announced in a matter-of-fact voice that at last, after so many years of hardship, they had reached their destination. Henson explained to Ootah, "We have found what we hunt." The Eskimo shrugged his shoulders, still unable to fully understand these strange outsiders from another part of the world. "There is nothing here," Ootah said. "Only ice."

An Eskimo family in Greenland converses and plays outside its tent, which is made from the skins of seals. During the summer, Eskimos often lived in tents instead of in igloos.

North Pole
Arctic Ocean
ELLESMERE Is.
GREENLAND
Iceland
Baffin Island
Hudson Bay

Henson and Peary's successful route to the North Pole.

With an American flag in his hand, Henson climbed to the top of a nearby pressure ridge. Peary snapped his picture. Then Henson helped set up camp. After a long night's sleep, the expedition headed home. Henson's exploring days were over.

The rest of Matthew Henson's life was frustrating in many ways. Peary was treated as a national hero, but Henson was slighted. Racist reporters asked Peary why he had allowed a Negro to accompany him to the North Pole. Peary, who was unwilling to share the credit for his achievement, made things worse with his answer. He had been forced to take Henson with him all the way, he said, because Henson was too ignorant to make it back to the ship on his own. This was completely unfair, of course, for many times it had been only Henson's courage and intelligence that saved the expedition from disaster. While Peary received large fees for giving lectures and was granted a rich pension from the government, Henson was forced to park cars in a Brooklyn garage to earn his living.

But Matthew Henson was not the kind of man to let bitterness ruin his life. He later got a good job with the U.S. Customs Bureau, and he lived a long, rich, full life until he died in 1955, at the age of 88. During his final years he took satisfaction in his own knowledge of all that he had achieved. If any doubted him, there was always the picture Peary had taken at the North Pole.

That photograph showed Matthew Henson, a black American, with the flag of his country in his hand at the top of the world. And anyone who doubted his achievements could always ask the Eskimos, who for years afterward told legends about a very great man named Miy Paluk. The Eskimos even added a new word to their language: The word *ahdoolo* came to stand for a very special kind of courage. It was used not only to mean bravery and endurance, but to mean the ability to face even the hardest work and the greatest challenge with hope and good spirits. It is a fitting word with which to remember Matthew Henson.

Triumph at the Pole: Atop an icy hill near the North Pole, Henson and his Eskimo friends hoist the American flag and several other banners.

S O U R C E

NATIONAL GEOGRAPHIC
world

Magazine

Standing Up for
ANTARCTICA

YOUNG EXPLORERS wave their expedition flags in Antarctica with Jacques-Yves Cousteau (in the red cap). They are, from the left, Elise Otzenberger, 12, Europe; Oko Joseph Shio, 12, Africa; Kelly Jean Matheson, 12, Australia; Cory Gillmer, 13, North America; Fumiko Matsumoto, 13, Asia; and Jeronimo Brunner, 12, South America.

Six students from six continents visited Antarctica last year with explorer Jacques-Yves Cousteau. The purpose of the expedition was to point out the need to protect Antarctica for future generations.

As they approached the continent by ship, the students saw icebergs glittering in the sun. Seals and whales bobbed in the icy waters.

Once ashore the explorers visited a penguin rookery, or nesting ground, and met scientists at research stations of Brazil, Poland, and the Soviet Union. They also saw the wreck of a ship that had spilled fuel in 1989, killing wildlife.

The students, each representing a continent, will never forget their journey or the sights and sounds of Antarctica. Kelly Matheson, 12, of Australia, remembers icebergs breaking off into the sea. "All night long, we could hear the ice cracking like thunder and falling into the water," she says.

Will Antarctica remain largely unspoiled in the future? These young people will do all they can to make sure it does.

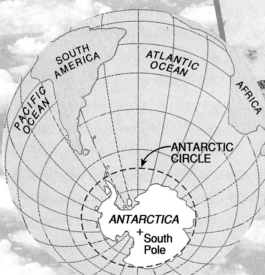

IN A PENGUIN ROOKERY, or nesting site, a snow-coated, Adélie chick waits for a meal. Parent penguins feed their young partly digested krill, which they bring back from the icy waters surrounding the continent of Antarctica.

Dr. Mae Jemison

Astronaut

An *astronaut* reaches for the stars.

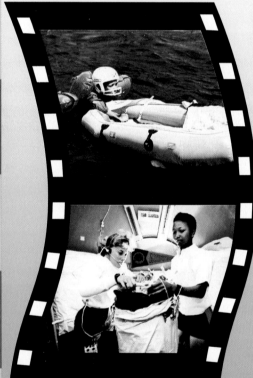

On September 12, 1992, a team of astronauts boarded the space shuttle *Endeavor*. Mission Control gave the final ten-second countdown: 3...2...1... Then the rockets ignited, and the shuttle zoomed into outer space. On board was Dr. Mae Jemison— physician, chemical engineer, and astronaut.

PROFILE

Name: Dr. Mae Jemison

Occupation: doctor, chemical engineer, astronaut, entrepreneur

Languages: English, Russian, Japanese, and Swahili

Hobbies: dance, weight training, reading history, photography

Childhood dream: to travel through outer space

UESTIONS
for Dr. Mae Jemison

Find out why **Dr. Jemison** *became* **an astronaut.**

 A space mission involves a lot of people working together. Would you say that teamwork is an important part of the process?

I think teamwork is important in anything that you do. To be an astronaut means working with a team. Each astronaut has a job to do while in space, and those jobs can be complicated. But the bulk of the work is done by the people who stay on the ground—the scientists and engineers who get the shuttle ready. We're all part of the same team.

 What was your job during the space shuttle flight?

 I was the science mission specialist. My job was to be the representative of the scientists on the ground who had designed the experiments. I was their eyes, ears, and hands. I did experiments to find out how the human body adapts to weightlessness.

 When did you decide that you wanted to become an astronaut?

As a child, I watched the Gemini and Apollo launches on television in the 1960s. When I watched the astronauts walk on the moon, I knew that I would go into space one day.

Q When did you start working toward your goal of joining the space program?

A I started working toward my goal when I was still in school. I got my degree in chemical engineering and then went on to become a doctor. In 1985 I decided to apply to NASA's astronaut program. I was accepted in 1987.

Q What advice would you give to kids who want to become astronauts?

A There are not enough spaces for everyone to become an astronaut. But all kinds of people are involved in making space exploration work, so remember you can always be involved. My advice is to find something that you like to do. Don't be limited by others who have a limited imagination.

Dr. Mae Jemison's Tips for Working Together as a Team

1 Share your ideas with the others on your team.

2 Remember that everyone is a part of the team.

3 Be willing to compromise.

THE BEST NEW THING

by Isaac Asimov
illustrated by Tom Leonard

AWARD
WINNING

Author

Rada lived on a little world, far out in space. Her father and her mother and her brother, Jonathan, lived there too. So did other men and women.

Rada was the only little girl on the little world. Jonny was the only little boy. They had lived there all their lives. Rada's father and other men worked on the spaceships. They made sure everything was all right before the spaceships went on their way back to Earth or to other planets. Rada and Jonny would watch them come and go.

They had a special place where they could stand and watch the ships come down. The ships came down slower and slower and then they stopped.

Rada and Jonny had to wear their space suits when they watched. There was no air on the little world, but inside their suits there was air and it was warm. Over their heads they wore a glass ball that they could see through.

When men and women came out of the spaceships, they would see Rada and Jonny. Then they would say, "Think of that! Children live here."

One of the men said, "Have you lived here all your life?"

Rada said, "Yes, I have. We both have."

The man said, "Would you like to see Earth someday? It is a big world."

Jonny asked, "Are things different on Earth?"

"Well, the sky is blue," said the man.

"I have never seen a blue sky," said Rada. "The sky is always black here."

"On Earth, it is blue, except at night," said the man. "It is warm on Earth and there is air everywhere. You don't have to wear a space suit on Earth."

Rada said, "That must be nice. I will ask my father if I can go to Earth."

She jumped high to see where her father was. She jumped very high, higher than the man—much higher than the man. When she was that high, she could see all around the spaceship. She did not see her father, so she knew he must be inside the spaceship.

She pushed a little button on her suit. Some air came out fast. It went s-s-s-s. That made her go down again. She came down very near the man.

The man said, "You do that very well."

Jonny said, "I can do it, too. See?"

He jumped high—and then made himself come down headfirst. He landed very softly.

The man laughed and said, "That is well done, too, but you could not do that on Earth."

Rada said, "Why not?"

"On Earth," said the man, "you can only jump a little way. Earth is so big, it holds you down. If you jump up, Earth pulls you down right away. And you could roll down any slanting place."

Then the man had to go into the spaceship again. Rada and Jonny waited for their father.

When their father came, Rada and Jonny went underground with him. Rada and Jonny and their father and mother lived inside the little world, in large, comfortable rooms.

It was warm and nice inside their home. There were books and toys and good things to eat. And there was air for them to breathe, so they could take off their big, clumsy space suits. Jonny and Rada liked to run around with not many clothes on. Of course, even indoors they couldn't run without bouncing high into the air, because the little world was too little to pull them down.

Jonny said, "Daddy, is it true that you don't have to wear a space suit on Earth?"

His father said, "Yes, it is. There is air on Earth, just like the air that we have to manufacture here so we can breathe in these rooms."

Jonny said, "And is the sky really blue there?"

"That's right," his father answered. "And there are white things in the sky called clouds. Sometimes drops of water come from the sky. That is rain."

Rada thought about this for a minute, and then she said, "If the ground has water on it, doesn't that make it slippery?"

Her father laughed, and then he said, "The rain doesn't stay on top of the ground. It sinks into the ground and helps to make the grass grow."

Rada knew about grass, because her father and mother had told her about it. But she liked to hear about it over and over again. So she said, "Tell me about grass again, Daddy."

"Grass is like a green carpet that grows on the ground. It is soft and very beautiful," he said.

"I would like to see it," said Rada. "And I would like to feel it too. Will we go to Earth someday, Daddy?"

"Oh yes, Rada," her father said. "Perhaps we can go soon."

Rada was so happy to hear this that she wanted to put her arms about her father. She walked up the wall to be near his head.

Rada could do that on her little world, because that world was too little to pull her down. She could walk on the wall or anywhere because her shoes were made to stick to everything.

When she walked on the wall, the wall was under her feet just like a floor. Her head was near her father's head now and she put her arms around him.

"Thank you, Daddy," she said.

Her father hugged her and said, "You know, if you were on Earth, you could not walk on the wall. Earth would pull you down."

Rada's mother came into the room. She pushed down on the floor with her feet. That made her move up. She came to a stop near the top of the room by pushing the air with her hand.

She held two containers. She said, "Rada! Jonny! Here is your milk."

When she let go of the containers, they stayed in the air.

"Oh good, I'm thirsty," Rada said. She pushed the wall with her feet and moved to the container. She opened the container and put a straw into the opening.

Jonny moved up into the air and came near the other container. He said, "I don't want to use a straw, Mommy. May I roll the milk into a ball?"

"All right, but be careful not to get any on your clothes," his mother said.

Jonny opened the container and shook it. The milk floated out and made a soft white ball. Some of it made little tiny balls. Jonny pushed the tiny balls with his finger and they all went back into the big white ball.

He pushed the air with his hands and moved his head very near the ball. He put his lips to it and sucked it in. It was fun to drink milk that way.

His father said "If you drank milk that way on Earth, it would get all over your clothes. You will have to remember many things like that when you are on Earth."

"Have I ever been there, Daddy?" asked Rada.

"Oh yes," said her father, "but you can't remember it because you were only a baby when you came here with Mommy and me. And Jonny wasn't even born. Now it will soon be time to go back to Earth. We will take you with us."

Rada moved to her father and put her head on top of his. Her feet were in the air. Jonny had finished his milk and he was moving around and around his father, pushing the air to make himself go.

"Can you see the stars on Earth, Daddy?" asked Rada. On their little world, they could always see the stars because the sky was always dark.

"Yes, you can," said her father. "Part of the time."

Rada and Jonny talked a long time about Earth. They could hardly sleep that night. They kept thinking about Earth.

There were so many new things on Earth to think about. There was air that was everywhere. There were the blue sky and the rain, the wind and the flowers. And there were birds and animals.

The next day their father showed them pictures of some of the new things. They saw that the ground could be flat in some places and hilly in others. Soon they would see and feel all these things for themselves.

There would be other boys and girls to play with on Earth. There would be so many new things to see and do.

But there was one new thing Rada especially wanted to do. She told Jonny about it and he wanted to do it too. They didn't tell their father or mother. It was something they had never done in all their lives. On Earth, they were going to find out what it felt like.

Rada and Jonny had to make themselves strong for living on Earth.

Her mother said, "Now, Rada, Earth is a big world. It will pull at you hard. You must be strong so that you can walk in spite of all that pull."

Jonny said, "Yes, Rada, you have to be as strong as I am."

But Mother said, "You will have to be stronger than you are now, too, Jonny."

There were springs on the wall in the exercise room. Rada and Jonny had to pull on them. They stood on the wall and pulled on the springs. They pulled and pulled. It took all their strength to move the springs.

"Pull hard the way I do," said Jonny. He was breathing fast from all that pulling.

Rada said, "When we get strong, we can go to Earth. We will see grass and flowers and trees. Most of all, we will find out about the new thing."

Jonny said, "Don't tell anybody."

They pulled very hard.

Their father was happy. "You are both getting very strong," he said. "You will like it on Earth."

One day a spaceship came and their father said, "This is the ship that will take us to Earth."

They all put on their space suits. Their father was ready to go. So was their mother. But Rada and Jonny were ready first.

Rada felt a little bit sorry. She would miss her little world. When they were getting into the spaceship, she turned and said, "Goodbye, little world. Maybe I will see you again someday." Then she jumped very high so she could see almost all of their side of the little world.

"Good-bye," she said again. "It is time for me to go to Earth now."

Jonny called her from the spaceship. "Come on, slowpoke. We're all waiting for you."

On the spaceship they went to their little room. It had chairs with seatbelts.

Their father said, "Let me put the seatbelts around you, children. They must hold you when the spaceship starts to move."

He fastened their seatbelts so they couldn't move. Then their father and mother sat in their own chairs and fastened their own seatbelts. The chairs were very soft.

Then the spaceship started to move. There was a big noise all through the ship and Rada and Jonny were pushed against the soft, soft chair. They were pushed harder and harder but the seatbelts kept everything all right.

"I'm not frightened," said Jonny. "Are you frightened, Rada?"

"Just a little bit," said Rada. She could see the little world as the ship moved away from it. The little world was smaller than ever. Soon it was just a dot and then all Rada could see were the stars.

"Can we see Earth, Daddy?" Jonny asked.

"It looks like a star from here. It's that bright one there," said his father.

"Look at Earth, Rada," said Jonny. He was very excited.

Rada looked at the bright star and was happy. Soon she would be on Earth and would know about the new thing. She knew Jonny was thinking about it, too.

"Wake up, Rada," said her father. "We are coming down to Earth. Jonny is awake already."

Rada opened her eyes. "Can we get out of the ship now, Daddy?"

"Soon, Rada," said her father. "You must wait a little while."

Rada looked out the window. Down below she could see a big, big world. She had never seen anything so very, very big. It was green and brown and lots of other colors too. She could see water, too, and that was blue.

Above all the green and brown and blue and other colors of the Earth was the sky.

Jonny said, "How big everything is!"

And Rada said, "How pretty everything is!"

They could hardly wait.

When the ship stopped, Rada took off her belt. She was the first one to get out of the chair. Jonny was second.

Jonny tried to walk. "The floor is holding my foot," he said.

"Pull harder," said his father.

Jonny did and at last he succeeded in lifting his foot from the floor.

"Aren't we going to put on our space suits?" asked Rada.

"Don't forget, we don't have to put on space suits on Earth," said her father.

"Oh, yes," said Rada. "That's one of the new things." She and Jonny were waiting for another new thing, too. They squeezed each other's hands but they didn't say anything.

They went down and down and down inside the ship to get to a little door that would let them out on the Earth. It was hard to walk, but they were beginning to get used to it.

The door opened and they all walked out. There was flat paving all around the spaceship, as there had been on the little world. But at the edge of the paving there was grass. There had been no grass on the little world.

"My," said Mother, "doesn't the air smell sweet?"

"Oh, yes," said Rada. She could feel the air moving. That was the wind. It blew her dress and her hair.

It was warm and the sun was very big and yellow.

Jonny said, "Look how big the sun is." The sun had looked much smaller from their little world.

"Don't look right at the sun," his father said quickly. "That would hurt your eyes."

"What is that sound?" asked Rada.

"It is a bird singing," said her mother.

Rada had never heard a bird singing. She had never felt the wind. She had never seen such a big sun and such bright sunlight.

These were all new things.

Now it was time for the best new thing of all. Now she would find out what it was really like.

She said, "Come on, Jonny."

Jonny said, "Look at the grass. And there's a little hill just like the one in the pictures. Let's try it."

Rada said, "Look, Mother. See how I can run."

It was hard to run because Earth pulled at her legs. She ran with all her might to the grassy hill. Jonny was running, too.

Jonny said, "I can run faster than you." But they reached the grass together. Both were breathing hard from running.

Then they came to the little hill and they climbed to the top. That was even harder than walking, but they made it. They looked at each other and laughed, and then they both lay down on the grass and rolled down the hill. When they reached the bottom, they stood up, laughing and breathing hard.

Their father and mother came to them.

"Are you hurt, children?" their father asked.

"You should not run like that till you are used to Earth's pull," said their mother.

"Oh, but we wanted to," said Rada. "We are so happy because we know, now, about the new thing. It is something we had never done before."

"What new thing?" asked her father.

"We rolled down the hill," said Rada. "We could never do that before, because our own little world never pulled us. But it was really fun. I think it's the best new thing of all."

"Yes," said Jonny, "that is the best new thing of all."

And they ran up to the top of the hill to try it again.

How to
Create a Team Profile

If you were going on an expedition, would you go all by yourself? Probably not. Depending on where you were going, you would want people along who have specific skills. You would want to create a team profile.

What is a team profile? A team profile is a list of job titles and the skills that are needed for each job. Different expeditions require different skills. For an archaeological expedition, a team profile might include an archaeologist, a medical doctor, and a photographer.

MEET YOUR CREW

Each crew member aboard the ship is called a specialist. Here's what each specialist does:

ENVIRONMENTAL CONTROL:
Keeps air breathable and comfortable; takes care of the fresh water supply.

METEOROLOGIST:
Keeps track of weather.

COMMUNICATIONS:
Maintains radio contact between crew members, ship, and command center.

BIOLOGIST:
Looks for life forms.

ENGINEER:
Keeps ship's engines and electronics working.

MEDICAL OFFICER:
Tends to the health and well-being of all crew members.

The team's work is divided among professionals.

Each team member has a job title.

Each job has important responsibilities.

A doctor is an important member of any team.

1 Choose an Adventure

Choose an adventure that interests your team. It could be a space mission, an underwater expedition, or an exciting idea of your own. Once your team has agreed on the goal of your expedition, decide where it will take place. Look at an atlas for ideas.

TOOLS

- atlas or globe

- reference books

- magazines and newspapers

- paper and pencil

- posterboard and markers

2 Make a Checklist

Once you've chosen an adventure, make a checklist of important skills your team will need. Think about the place you are going. How will you get there? What will the environment be like? Use reference books, magazines, and newspapers to research the place and the skills needed to survive there. This research will help you write your skills checklist.

3 Choose a Job Title

After your team decides what skills will be needed on the expedition, make a list of job titles. Next to each job title, describe the skills and responsibilities of that job. Then, have each team member pick a job title from the list. Discuss why the role of each team member is important to the success of the expedition.

Tips
• Use maps, reference books, and magazines to help you think of adventure possibilities.
• Do some research! Read about people who have already been on your adventure. What kind of specialists were on the team? What problems and challenges did they face?

4 Present Your Team Profile

Create a team poster. Make a poster with drawings or photos of each crew member. Underneath each picture put the team member's job title and a description of duties. Draw a picture or a map of the place your expedition is going to. Be sure to include interesting facts that your team discovered while doing research. Present your team poster to the rest of your class.

If You Are Using a Computer ...

Write the job title and a description of each team member's skills on the computer. Print it out and use it on your poster. Be creative with the font sizes and styles. You may also want to use the Record Tools to describe your job on the team.

THINK

Why is it important that team members cooperate with each other if they all have different jobs?

Dr. Mae Jemison
Astronaut ▶

Science Search

Learn how one
tree in the rain
forest provides
food and shelter
for many animals.

Investigate the
world beneath
the sea with
marine biologist
Eugenie Clark.

Find out how
you can become
a member of the
Jason Project.

PROJECT

Research an interesting place,
and give a multimedia show
about it.

TAKE A TRIP
THAT'S OUT
OF THIS WORLD.

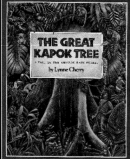

THE GREAT KAPOK TREE

A TALE OF THE AMAZON RAIN FOREST

by Lynne Cherry

AWARD WINNING Book

In the Amazon rain forest it is always hot, and in that heat everything grows, and grows, and grows. The tops of the trees in the rain forest are called the canopy. The canopy is a sunny place that touches the sky. The animals that live there like lots of light. Colorful parrots fly from tree to tree. Monkeys leap from branch to branch. The bottom of the rain forest is called the understory. The animals that live in the understory like darkness. There, silent snakes curl around hanging vines. Graceful jaguars watch and wait.

And in this steamy environment the great Kapok tree shoots up through the forest and emerges above the canopy.

This is the story of a community of animals that live in one such tree in the rain forest.

Two men walked into the rain forest. Moments before, the forest had been alive with the sounds of squawking birds and howling monkeys. Now all was quiet as the creatures watched the two men and wondered why they had come.

The larger man stopped and pointed to a great Kapok tree. Then he left.

The smaller man took the ax he carried and struck the trunk of the tree. Whack! Whack! Whack! The sounds of the blows rang through the forest. The wood of the tree was very hard. Chop! Chop! Chop! The man wiped off the sweat that ran down his face and neck. Whack! Chop! Whack! Chop!

Soon the man grew tired. He sat down to rest at the foot of the great Kapok tree. Before he knew it, the heat and hum of the forest had lulled him to sleep.

A boa constrictor lived in the Kapok tree. He slithered down its trunk to where the man was sleeping. He looked at the gash the ax had made in the tree. Then the huge snake slid very close to the man and hissed in his ear: "Senhor, this tree is a tree of miracles. It is my home, where generations of my ancestors have lived. Do not chop it down."

A bee buzzed in the sleeping man's ear: "Senhor, my hive is in this Kapok tree, and I fly from tree to tree and flower to flower collecting pollen. In this way I pollinate the trees and flowers throughout the rain forest. You see, all living things depend on one another."

A troupe of monkeys scampered down from the canopy of the Kapok tree. They chattered to the sleeping man: "Senhor, we have seen the ways of man. You chop down one tree, then come back for another and another. The roots of these great trees will wither and die, and there will be nothing left to hold the earth in place. When the heavy rains come, the soil will be washed away and the forest will become a desert."

A toucan, a macaw, and a cock-of-the-rock flew down from the canopy. "Senhor!" squawked the toucan, "you must not cut down this tree. We have flown over the rain forest and see what happens once you begin to chop down the trees. Many people settle on the land. They set fires to clear the underbrush and soon the forest disappears. Where once there was life and beauty only black and smoldering ruins remain."

A bright and small tree frog crawled along the edge of a leaf. In a squeaky voice he piped in the man's ear: "Senhor, a ruined rain forest means ruined lives . . . many ruined lives. You will leave many of us homeless if you chop down this great Kapok tree."

A jaguar had been sleeping along a branch in the middle of the tree. Because his spotted coat blended into the dappled light and shadows of the understory, no one had noticed him. Now he leapt down and padded silently over to the sleeping man. He growled in his ear: "Senhor, the Kapok tree is home to many birds and animals. If you cut it down, where will I find my dinner?"

Four tree porcupines swung down from branch to branch and whispered to the man: "Senhor, do you know what we animals and humans need in order to live? Oxygen. And, Senhor, do you know what trees produce? Oxygen! If you cut down the forests you will destroy that which gives us all life."

Several anteaters climbed down the Kapok tree with their young clinging to their backs. The unstriped anteater said to the sleeping man: "Senhor, you are chopping down this tree with no thought for the future. And surely you know that what happens tomorrow depends upon what you do today. The big man tells you to chop down a beautiful tree. He does not think of his own children, who tomorrow must live in a world without trees."

A three-toed sloth had begun climbing down from the canopy when the men first appeared. Only now did she reach the ground. Plodding ever so slowly over to the sleeping man, she spoke in her deep and lazy voice: "Senhor, how much is beauty worth? Can you live without it? If you destroy the beauty of the rain forest, on what would you feast your eyes?"

A child from the Yanomamo tribe who lived in the rain forest knelt over the sleeping man. He murmured in his ear: "Senhor, when you awake, please look upon us all with new eyes."

The man awoke with a start. Before him stood the rain forest child, and all around him, staring, were the creatures who depended upon the great Kapok tree. What wondrous and rare animals they were!

The man looked about and saw the sun streaming through the canopy. Spots of bright light glowed like jewels amidst the dark green forest. Strange and beautiful plants seemed to dangle in the air, suspended from the great Kapok tree.

The man smelled the fragrant perfume of their flowers. He felt the steamy mist rising from the forest floor. But he heard no sound, for the creatures were strangely silent.

The man stood and picked up his ax. He swung back his arm as though to strike the tree. Suddenly he stopped. He turned and looked at the animals and the child.

He hesitated. Then he dropped the ax and walked out of the rain forest.

emerald
tree boa

scarlet
macaw

toucan

Brazilian
tree frog

coati

scamander

red-necke
tanage

tree
frog

three-toed sloth

urania
butterfly

cock-of-the-rock

tree
porcupine

mother &
baby tapir

ARCTIC OCEAN

GREENLAND

NORTH
AMERICA

EUROPE

ATLANTIC

AFRICA

Central
America

CARIBBEAN
SEA

THE
AMAZON RAIN FOREST

Rio Negro   Manaus
AMAZON RIVER

Brazil

OCEAN

Equator

Madaga

SOUTH
AMERICA

PACIFIC
OCEAN

☐ today's rain forests
☐ original extent of rain forests

Tropical Rain Forests

mother & baby
giant anteater

baby
hoatzin

poison
arrow
frog

Vindula
arsinoë
butterfly

Amazonian
katydid

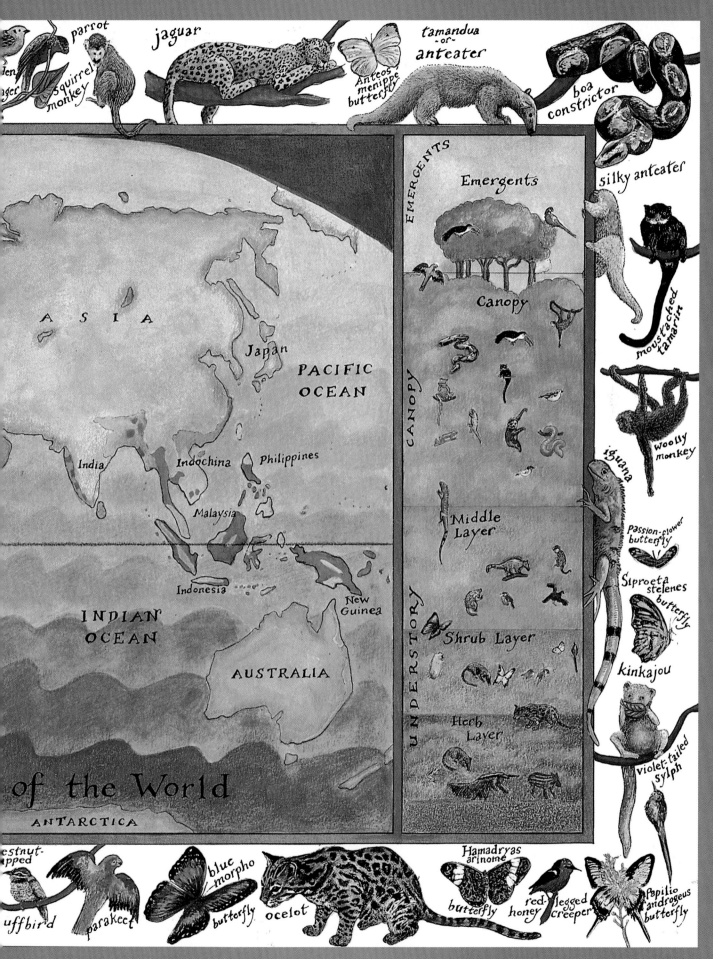

parrot

jaguar

tamandua
~or~
anteater

Anteos
menippe
butterfly

boa
constrictor

Squirrel
monkey

silky anteater

EMERGENTS

Emergents

moustached
tamarin

Canopy

CANOPY

woolly
monkey

iguana

Middle
Layer

passion-flower
butterfly

UNDERSTORY

Siproeta
stelenes
butterfly

Shrub Layer

kinkajou

Herb
Layer

violet-tailed
Sylph

A S I A

Japan

PACIFIC
OCEAN

India

Indochina

Philippines

Malaysia

Indonesia

New
Guinea

INDIAN
OCEAN

AUSTRALIA

of the World

ANTARCTICA

estnut-
pped

uffbird

parakeet

blue
morpho
butterfly

ocelot

Hamadryas
arinome
butterfly

red-
honey

legged
creeper

Papilio
androgeus
butterfly

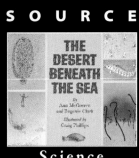

FROM

AWARD
WINNING

Author

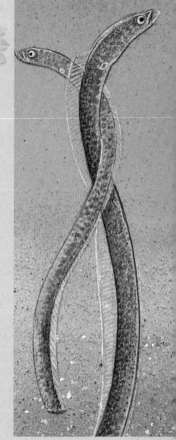

THE DESERT BENEATH THE SEA

By
Ann McGovern
and Eugenie Clark

Illustrated by
Craig Phillips

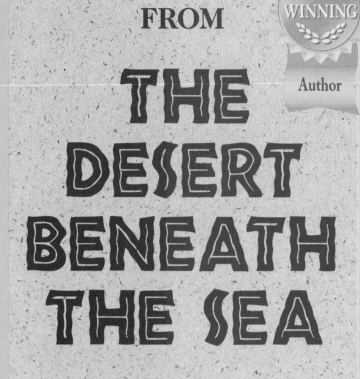

How Marine Biologists Study the Undersea Desert

Marine biologist Eugenie Clark is known as the Shark Lady. She studies sharks all over the world. But she is also interested in the tiny creatures who live in the desert beneath the sea.

A scientist like Eugenie Clark studies fish in many different ways. As a young girl, she studied fish in an aquarium at home. Now she goes on expeditions to observe the creatures in their homes in the sea. She goes scuba diving to study their behavior firsthand. Many people enjoy diving with her—students, her grown children, other scientists and diving friends, including author Ann McGovern.

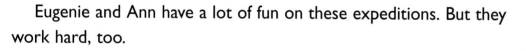

Eugenie and Ann have a lot of fun on these expeditions. But they work hard, too.

They learn to lie quietly on the sea bottom, careful not to disturb the creatures they are studying.

Ann takes notes for her books and Eugenie records her findings. They write with a pencil tied to a plastic slate or on special underwater paper held to a clipboard with two rubber bands.

Eugenie and her scuba-diving friends watch how the creatures behave . . . how they act alone and with other sand dwellers . . . how they fight, feed, and mate . . . how the seasons and the sun and moon and currents affect them. They study the creatures at sunrise, at dusk, and in the dark of night.

Eugenie also studies the kind of water and sand in which the creatures live. She spends many hours in libraries and museums all over the world. She reads information by other scientists.

Back in her lab at the University of Maryland where she is a professor of Zoology, Eugenie does further study. She examines fish preserved in alcohol by *dissecting*, or cutting them open. She studies tiny parts of them under microscopes.

She counts the rays in each fin and the scales on their bodies. She measures many parts of the fish.

She examines what remains in the fishes' stomachs to find out what they eat. Sometimes she has to play detective. From only a few fish scales or bones, she tries to figure out the kind of food that was eaten.

In a notebook, she records all her information, called *data*. This data can also be put into a computer, revealing other fish facts. As she writes her findings, she analyzes and studies the computer images.

Her data is published in scientific magazines and books for other scientists to read. Sometimes she writes for popular magazines, like *National Geographic*. Her stories are illustrated with beautiful photographs.

If You Joined an Underwater Expedition

Suppose you were a scuba diver and were invited to take part in an underwater study. You would be one of fourteen people—including Ann McGovern—who volunteered to live on a dive boat for a week to study the sand tilefish of the Caribbean Sea.

The leaders of the expedition—Eugenie Clark and Joan Rabin—would give you jobs to do. You would help them try to find answers to many questions about the sand tilefish.

How deep down do these fish build their burrows? What are they made of? Does each fish build its burrow alone or with other tilefishes? Why are the tops of burrows built so big? Is it to show off? Is it to build an artificial reef to attract their food?

Coral reefs around the world are being damaged in shallow waters where people drop their trash—sometimes right in the tilefish's territory. How does the tilefish react to this?

Your first job would be to scuba dive to locate the sand tilefish. Its pale color makes it hard to spot when it hovers above the sandy bottom. You would learn to tell males from females. Males are larger and develop streamers on their tails. They behave differently from females.

Tilefish homes, called *burrows*, are easy to locate because of the mountains of coral rubble piled on top. Some of them are over eight feet across. Juvenile tilefish build small burrows. Once you find a burrow, you mark it with a plastic marker with your initials and a number. All week, you would study that area and the tilefish that live there. You would see that only one tilefish lives in each burrow.

You would measure the size of the roof mounds and the distances between them. You use a compass and a cotton string that is knotted in measured lengths. After each scuba dive, you give your information to Eugenie or Joan. They record your observations in a scientific way. They make detailed drawings and maps of the whole area. Your observations would be part of a scientific study.

Another job would be to help Joan *excavate*, or take apart, a large roof mound. These are made mostly of pieces of broken coral. A tilefish can easily build its burrow and roof mound again.

First Joan divides the large mound into four parts with her diving knife, the way you might divide a pie. One quarter, or *quadrant*, would be studied. You pick up the coral pieces carefully and put them into your collecting bag. When the bag is filled, a lift bag is inflated to bring the heavy rubble up to the boat.

The coral rubble is weighed and sorted. You would work on the back deck, sorting the hundreds of coral rubble pieces by size and shape and texture. The job might take all afternoon. Your back would get very tired, bending over the piles of rubble on the deck. Mixed in with the coral rubble, you might find surprises—fish teeth, bits of glass, and other trash.

A photographer takes pictures of the tilefish underwater. Now he photographs the rubble on the deck.

You would learn many things on this expedition. You would see tilefish at different depths—from eight feet to 168 feet! You would see groups of little yellowhead jawfish that make their burrows nearby. You might wonder why the jawfish live so close to the tilefish. Scientists wonder, too—but no one has been able to come up with a scientific reason, so far.

On many dives, you would see a tilefish pick up a piece of coral in its mouth. It would swim up to a big mound. Yet the tilefish makes its mound even bigger by adding another piece of coral on top! Scientists are still investigating the reasons why tilefish keep building.

Divers check up on the fish at night, too. When the sun sets, the tilefish cover the openings to their burrows by fanning the sand with their tails. Then they dive through the soft, new sand that closes over them. Here they sleep until morning, protected from danger.

Joan and Eugenie want to see what happens if a burrow entrance is blocked. They ask you to help. Tilefish move objects by carrying them or dragging them with their mouths. At the entrance of one burrow, you place a red plastic checker. At the second, you block the entrance with a golf ball. You put a clothespin in front of the last burrow.

You watch to see if the tilefish moves them. The red checker doesn't completely block the entrance so the tilefish simply ignores it and slips in and out of the burrow.

The golf ball is too round and smooth for the tilefish to get hold of in its mouth, so it does not use that burrow opening again.

And the clothespin? The tilefish can pick it up easily and move it to the top of its burrow.

Probably the most important fact you would learn is that sand tilefish can make a home out of almost anything. If there is no coral around, they use pieces of a light bulb, parts of shipwrecks, bits of glass, a fishnet or a clothespin—even little pieces of diving equipment. They seem to use anything that might have dropped into the sea.

Sometimes sand tilefish make their home in plastic pipes or under wooden boards that are lying on the sandy bottom. It seems they can live in almost any kind of shelter.

A Mystery Fish

One day, Eugenie and her friend David Shen were diving in the Red Sea. They were studying razorfish when David noticed a strange fish swimming by. David had never seen such a fish before.

It looked like a tiny jawfish with a big head and four dark patches on its back. It was a female with her belly bulging with eggs. He took many pictures of the fish.

David motioned to Eugenie. She swam over to the mystery fish. She, too, had never seen anything like it. They collected it in a plastic bag and brought it to the surface. They kept it alive in a bucket of seawater and brought it to David Fridman at the aquarium. Surely he would be able to identify the fish.

But David Fridman didn't know what it was, either. By chance, a scientist from a museum in Germany happened to be visiting the Red Sea. He got very excited when he saw the strange little fish and asked to take it back to his museum.

It turned out to be a new species. He preserved the fish by pickling it in a jar with special chemicals. He described it in a scientific paper and named it *Stalix davidsheni,* after David Shen.

David Shen says today, "I often wonder what that little fish was doing, swimming over the sand. It was not the usual jawfish behavior. Jawfish usually build their burrows in sand and rubble. They almost never wander far from their homes. Was this rare fish looking for its mate?"

Since that day in 1984, no other *Stalix davidsheni* has been seen, but Eugenie and David keep looking.

David Shen joined Eugenie and Ann McGovern on a Red Sea trip in 1980 because he wanted to learn about fish. It was his first expedition. Since then he has become an expert underwater photographer, and some of his pictures have been on magazine covers.

David has also become an expert on many kinds of fish. He became fascinated with the desert beneath the sea and produced a movie about it. He helped Eugenie map the largest colony of garden eels in the world. He knows fish by their scientific names.

If you help scientists, like David does, perhaps some day, you, too, will have a fish named after you!

THE JASON PROJECT

Passport to Adventure

The Jason Project is named after a character in Greek mythology. In Greek myths, Jason was the first great explorer to sail the seas. His ship was called the Argo, so the sea-going members of the Jason Project are called "argonauts."

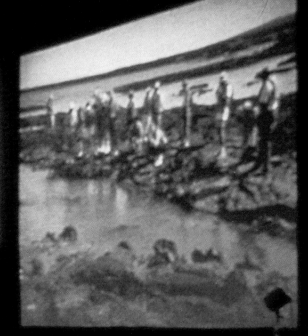

Picture this. You are at the controls of a deep-sea submersible. Your robot-like vehicle has dived down more than a mile under the ocean's surface. All around you, the sea is pitch black, except where your vehicle's floodlights pierce the darkness. You can see tiny, brightly colored sea animals dancing through the light beams.

Cautiously, you steer your way into a deep undersea canyon. You enter what seems to be a mysterious new planet. All around you, giant tube worms sway. Huge crabs crawl by in slow motion. You are at the bottom of the ocean, seeing what few humans have ever seen.

Finally, it's time for you to leave. You turn over the controls to another pilot. Then you turn around. Watching you are your classmates, teachers, and a big audience. You are not underwater at all. You have just been on an electronic field trip as a member of the Jason Project team!

The Jason Project gives students all over the world a chance to be part of an underwater discovery team. The project is the brainchild of Dr. Robert Ballard, an oceanographer and deep-sea explorer, who discovered and visited the wreck of the *Titanic*. After making his famous discovery in a manned submersible, Ballard got thousands of letters from students. "I realized that we could put this incredible robot technology to work to excite students about the thrills of scientific discovery," he says.

Ballard has set up a team of scientists, computer experts, and explorers to work with young people interested in underwater exploration. A complex communications network allows students to become part of Ballard's discovery team.

This is how it works. Scientists aboard a research ship send a remote-operated robot vehicle named *Jason* down into the ocean depths. Pictures from the robot are transmitted from the research ship to a satellite. From there, they are beamed to auditoriums across the United States.

Lucky students in the audience become "pilots" and sit at control panels where they can talk to the scientists and drive the robot vehicle. The audiences can watch on huge screens set up in the auditoriums. A few young people are even luckier! For each expedition of the Jason Project, several student "argonauts" are chosen. They accompany the scientists on board the research ship and become members of the exploration team.

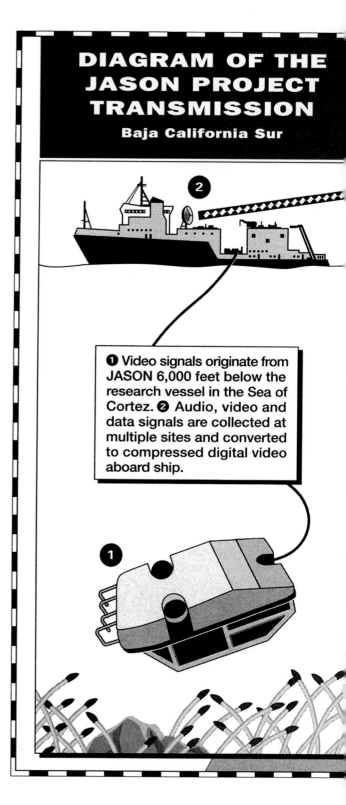

DIAGRAM OF THE JASON PROJECT TRANSMISSION
Baja California Sur

❶ Video signals originate from JASON 6,000 feet below the research vessel in the Sea of Cortez. ❷ Audio, video and data signals are collected at multiple sites and converted to compressed digital video aboard ship.

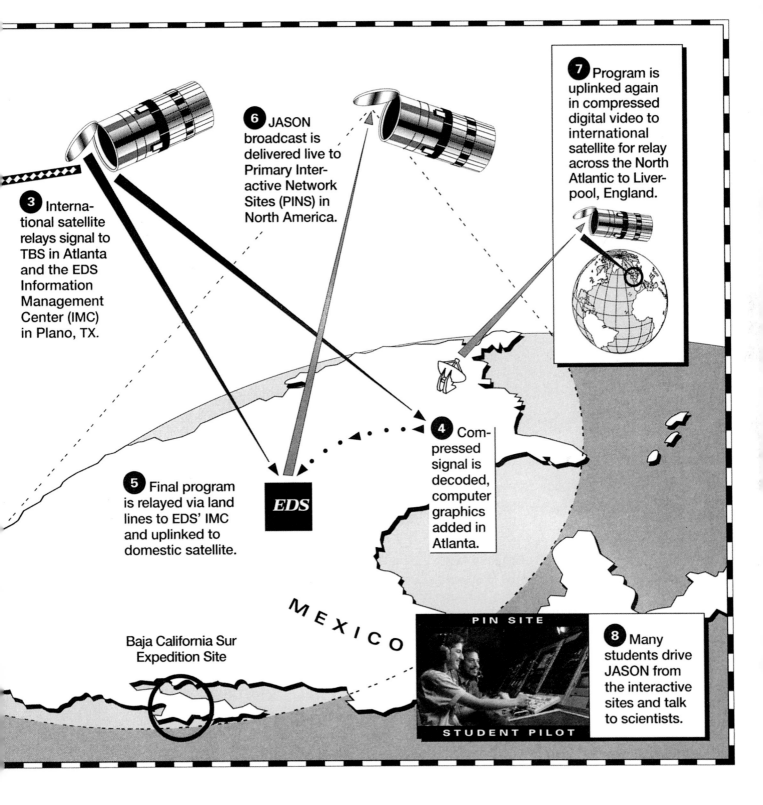

3 International satellite relays signal to TBS in Atlanta and the EDS Information Management Center (IMC) in Plano, TX.

6 JASON broadcast is delivered live to Primary Interactive Network Sites (PINS) in North America.

7 Program is uplinked again in compressed digital video to international satellite for relay across the North Atlantic to Liverpool, England.

5 Final program is relayed via land lines to EDS' IMC and uplinked to domestic satellite.

EDS

4 Compressed signal is decoded, computer graphics added in Atlanta.

MEXICO

Baja California Sur Expedition Site

PIN SITE

STUDENT PILOT

8 Many students drive JASON from the interactive sites and talk to scientists.

TEAMWORK TIPS

It definitely takes teamwork to make the Jason Project work. Two team members, Ernie Radowick and Christina Torruella give these tips for successful teamwork:

HAVE A MISSION EVERYONE BELIEVES IN. The mission of the Jason Project is to excite students about science and technology and get them involved in scientific discovery. "The feedback we get from students is my biggest satisfaction," says Radowick.

KEEP FOCUSED. "Everyone should have a specific task," says Torruella. "The danger is spreading yourself too thin," she warns. "Ask yourself, what do I have to do to accomplish my job. Then do it."

MAKE THE SUCCESS OF THE PROJECT YOUR GOAL. "The key is dedicated people who are willing to do whatever it takes for the project to succeed," says Radowick.

ENJOY WHAT YOU DO. Torruella gives this advice: "If you enjoy what you are doing, you will always succeed."

THE JASON PROJECT VOYAGES

The Jason Project has taken fantastic voyages all over the globe. Almost 1.5 million students have joined the project scientists on these journeys of discovery.

VOYAGE I — MAY 1989

The destination was the Mediterranean Sea.
A robot vehicle photographed the wreck of a Roman ship
that sank over 1,600 years ago.

VOYAGE II — MAY 1990

The Jason Project traveled to Lake Ontario.
It sent down a robot to view the wrecks of two ships that
sank during the War of 1812, a conflict between the
United States and Great Britain.

VOYAGE III — DECEMBER 1991

The team journeyed to the Galápagos Islands
in the Pacific Ocean, where scientists studied wildlife
on the islands and below the sea.

VOYAGE IV — MARCH 1993

In the Sea of Cortez, scientists
photographed tube worms and watched migrating whales.
The three-person submarine, the *Turtle*, was used
for underwater exploration.

VOYAGE V — MARCH 1994

Scientists explored the rain forest of Belize
while a robot vehicle explored sea life in the second
largest barrier reef in the Western Hemisphere.

How to Create a
Multimedia Presentation

Bring your *team's* **journey** to *life* **with** *words* **and** pictures.

If you rocketed into space, how could you share the excitement of the journey? One way is through a multi-media presentation. A multimedia presentation uses words, pictures, sound effects, and music to make an experience come alive. The idea for a presentation can start with a script. Then pictures, sound effects, lighting, models, and anything else can be added.

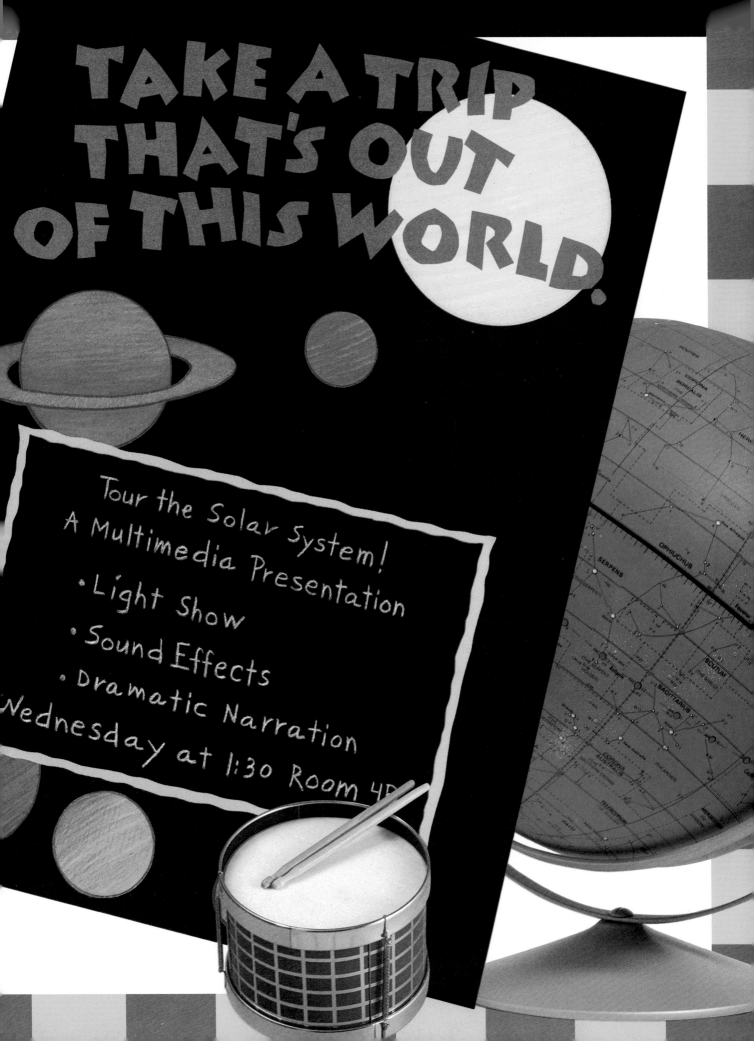

Your multimedia presentation will tell about an exciting place. So, first your team needs to choose a location. Pick a place that you want to learn more about. It can be as far away as Mars or as near as a location you can visit. Once you've chosen the place, it's time to gather facts and pictures for your show. Have each team member check a different source. Use atlases, travel books, magazines, encyclopedias, and newspapers. Team members can share their findings with the group.

TOOLS

- paper and pencil
- glue or tape
- colored markers
- magazine and newspaper pictures
- reference books and travel magazines
- tape recorder (optional)

Tips
- Use several different kinds of pictures and props in your show, such as original drawings, photographs, maps, and a globe.
- If you want to use a picture or map from a reference book, someone in the group can make a drawing or trace the original.
- If your pictures are small, mount them onto a posterboard. This will help them stand out.

The white lines show the Big Dipper, the Little Dipper, and the North Star.

Sun

Mercury

Venus

The Solar System

Earth

Spacecraft have already taken pictures of many of the planets that revolve around our sun. Perhaps someday you will be able to visit one of the other eight planets in our solar system. How exciting that would be!

Mars

Jupiter

Saturn

Uranus

Neptune

Pluto

2 Organize Your Material

Gather the materials you'll need for your show. Here are some things you may want to include.

- Captions: Write captions under all the pictures. Decide as a group what the captions will say.

- A Script: If you want, write a script and include stage directions.

- Music and Sound Effects: If you can borrow a tape recorder, some members of your team can record music or sound effects.

- A Model: Create a model to use in your presentation.

How Am I Doing?

Before you put your presentation together, take a few minutes to answer these questions with your group.

- Did we pick exciting, colorful pictures?

- Have we found interesting facts to go with our pictures?

- Did we decide how to organize our presentation?

- Do we need a script to go with our presentation?

3 Put It All Together

As a team, decide how to present your show. Here are some ideas. Tape your pictures together on a long sheet of paper. Two team members can unroll the paper while another team member reads the captions or the script. Mount several pictures onto pieces of posterboard. Narrate your trip while playing your music or a sound effects tape, if you made one. If you want a spotlight, try using a flashlight and dimming the lights. Think of different ways to perform your show, and then choose one.

Our solar system is part of an enormous group of stars called a galaxy.

The closer a planet is to the Sun, the shorter the year. Mercury is the closet planet to the Sun and has a year that is 88 Earth-days long.

The Moon is much smaller and lighter than the Earth.

4 Present Your Multimedia Show

Before you perform your show in front of the class, you may want to rehearse it a few times. Every team member should take part in the performance. While you are rehearsing, you may think of other things to add to your performance. Remember to discuss any changes with the rest of the team. When it's time to perform, speak up so your classmates will hear you. At the end of your performance, don't forget to have your team take a bow.

If You Are Using a Computer ...

Create your multimedia presentation on the computer. Choose photographs and clip art to show each stage of your team's journey. Use the Record Tools to narrate your presentation. Have fun adding music and sound effects. Then present your journey on the computer, using the Slide Show Tools.

The sun is 900,000 miles across and the temperature at its center is 15 million degrees centigrade.

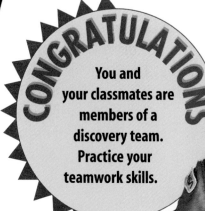

CONGRATULATIONS

You and your classmates are members of a discovery team. Practice your teamwork skills.

Dr. Mae Jemison
Astronaut ▶

Glossary

Arc·tic (ärk′tik) *noun*
The region lying north of the Arctic Circle.

as·tro·naut
(as′trə nôt′) *noun*
A person who is trained to fly in a spacecraft.

Word History

Astronaut is a compound of two Greek words: *astron,* which means "star," and *nautes,* which means "sailor." So an astronaut is a sailor among the stars.

---

bon·net (bon′it) *noun*
A hat with a wide brim and ribbons that tie under the chin.

buz·zards
(buz′ərdz) *noun*
Large birds with dark feathers, broad wings, and heads without feathers. ▲ **buzzard**

ca·noe·ing
(kə nōō′ing) *verb*
Paddling or traveling in a light narrow boat called a canoe. ▲ canoe

can·o·py
(kan′ə pē) *noun*
The tops of the trees in the rain forest.

com·pass
(kum′pəs) *noun*
An instrument that shows directions, such as north, south, east, and west. The hiker carried a *compass.*

cor·al reefs
(kôr′əl rēfs′) *noun*
Lines or strips of coral lying at or near the surface of the ocean. Many kinds of fish live among the *coral reefs.*
▲ **coral reef**

deep-sea
(dēp sē′) *adjective*
Having to do with the deeper parts of the sea.

ex·ca·vate
(eks′kə vāt′) *verb*
To dig a hole; to take apart. She helped the scientist *excavate* the pottery.

Thesaurus

excavate
dig
extract
quarry

find·ings
(fīn′dingz) *noun*
Conclusions reached after observation and research. When the experiment was over, she analyzed her *findings.*
▲ **finding**

astronaut

flax (flaks) *noun*
A kind of plant that has blue flowers, the seeds of which are used to make linseed oil.

freeze-dried (frēz′drīd′) *verb*
Processed a substance, such as food, by drying it in a frozen state under a high vacuum, so that it will keep for a long time.
▲ **freeze-dry**

frost·bit·ten (frôst′bit′n) *adjective*
Injured by exposure to extreme cold. The mountain climber's *frostbitten* fingers were numb.

huge (hyo͞oj) *adjective*
Of a very great size; enormous.

jag·uar (jag′ wär) *noun*
A large wild cat with brownish-yellow fur and black spots, similar to a leopard.

ka·pok tree (kā′pok trē′) *noun*
A kind of silk-cotton tree that grows in the Amazon rain forest.

launch·es (lônch′ iz) *noun*
The act of sending off space shuttles or rockets into outer space. She watched two space shuttle *launches* on TV.
▲ **launch**

ma·rine bi·ol·o·gist (mə rēn′ bī ol′ə jist) *noun*
Scientist who studies living things that make their home in the sea.

mead·ow·lark (med′ō lärk′) *noun*
A songbird with a yellow breast marked with a black V.

out·doors·men (out dôrz′ mən) *noun*
People who spend a lot of time outdoors, doing activities such as camping and hiking.
▲ **outdoorsman**

jaguar

a	add	o͝o	took	ə =
ā	ace	o͞o	pool	a in *above*
â	care	u	up	e in *sicken*
ä	palm	û	burn	i in *possible*
e	end	yo͞o	fuse	o in *melon*
ē	equal	oi	oil	u in *circus*
i	it	ou	pout	
ī	ice	ng	ring	
o	odd	th	thin	
ō	open	t͟h	this	
ô	order	zh	vision	

Glossary

pad·dock
(pad´ək) *noun*
A fenced area where horses exercise or graze. He fed an apple to the horse in the *paddock*.

pet·ti·coat
(pet´ē kōt´) *noun*
A kind of slip worn under a skirt or dress.

plan·et (plan´it) *noun*
Any of the nine large bodies in the solar system that revolve around the sun. Mars is a *planet*.

Word History

The word **planet** comes from the Greek word *planetai*. Ancient astronomers observed that while most stars stayed fixed in one place, a few of them would change position. They called these moving stars *planetai*, which means "wanderers."

po·lar (pō´lər) *adjective*
Of or near the South or North Pole.

prai·rie (prâr´ē) *noun*
A large area of flat or slightly rolling grasslands.

pres·sure ridges
(presh´ər rijəs) *noun*
Raised strips of ice and snow formed by the force of two bodies of ice crashing together.
▲ **pressure ridge**

quest (kwest) *noun*
An adventurous expedition. The prospector was on a *quest* for gold.

Thesaurus

quest
search
adventure
mission

rain for·est
(rān´fôr´ist) *noun*
A tropical forest, usually in an area that has a high annual rainfall.

Fact File

The temperature in a **rain forest** stays at about 80° F all year long. An average of 100 to 200 inches of rain falls throughout the year. The ground or floor of the rain forest is in almost total shade.

sci·en·tist
(sī´ən tist) *noun*
A person who is a specialist in science, especially the natural sciences.

sloth (slôth) *noun*
A slow-moving, tree-dwelling mammal with claws like hooks that inhabits the tropical forests of South and Central America.

Fact File

The **sloth** moves so slowly on the ground that it only covers about 6.5 feet every minute. In the trees, the sloth moves a little faster, sometimes covering as much as 10 feet in a minute.

sloth

space mis•sion
(spās′ mish′ən) *noun*
A project that a group of specialists is sent to do in space.

space shut•tle
(spās′ shut′l) *noun*
An airplane-like spacecraft designed to transport people and cargo between Earth and space.

space suit
(spās′ sōōt′) *noun*
A pressurized suit worn by astronauts that controls temperature and supplies them with oxygen.

space•ships
(spās′ ships) *noun*
Vehicles used for space travel.

sub•mers•i•ble
(səb mûr′sə bəl) *noun*
A vessel built to operate under water, usually a submarine.

tile•fish (tīl′fish′) *noun*
A large fish with yellow spots on its body found in the deep waters of the Atlantic.

tou•can (tōō′kan) *noun*
A brightly colored tropical bird with a large beak.

tum•ble•weeds
(tum′bəl wēds′) *noun*
Plants that break away from their roots in the autumn and are blown by the wind.
▲ tumbleweed

un•der•sto•ry
(un′dər stôr′ē) *noun*
A layer of shrubs and trees that only grow from 10 to 50 feet above the floor of a rain forest.

weight•less•ness
(wāt′lis′nes) *noun*
The state of having little or no weight because of the lack of gravity.

white wa•ter
(hwīt′ wô′tər) *noun*
Foaming, frothy water as in whitecaps and rapids.

wil•der•ness
(wil′dər nis) *noun*
A wild place or region that is uninhabited.

toucan

a	add	ōō	took	ə =
ā	ace	ōō	pool	a in *above*
â	care	u	up	e in *sicken*
ä	palm	û	burn	i in *possible*
e	end	yōō	fuse	o in *melon*
ē	equal	oi	oil	u in *circus*
i	it	ou	pout	
ī	ice	ng	ring	
o	odd	th	thin	
ō	open	th	this	
ô	order	zh	vision	

Authors & Illustrators

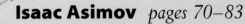

Isaac Asimov *pages 70–83*

This author has written more science and science-fiction books than any other writer. Now, even fifty years after some of his books were first published, they are still considered the best of their kind. His nonfiction work was also popular because he could write clear explanations of difficult subjects. He once said, "I'm on fire to explain, and happiest when it's something reasonably intricate, which I can make clear step by step." Isaac Asimov died in 1992.

Lynne Cherry *pages 90–103*

To research the illustrations and the text for *The Great Kapok Tree*, Lynne Cherry traveled to the Amazon rain forest in Brazil. As she sat by a jungle stream, a group of monkeys swung through the trees and a hummingbird hovered only a foot away! By writing the book, she hoped to give her readers a glimpse into a beautiful and marvelous world, one that is being destroyed at an alarming rate.

Eugenie Clark   *pages 104–115*

When Eugenie Clark was a little girl, living in New York City, she became interested in sharks. Every weekend, she spent hours at the city's aquarium. She never doubted she'd grow up to become a scientist. Today, many people call her "The Shark Lady" because she has made so many important discoveries about these fish.

Patricia MacLachlan   *pages 30–47*

This author was an avid reader as a child. She often read a whole book on the way home from the library— with her mother guiding her across streets and down curbs! Her father would act out parts in books she was reading, making them come to life. Family stories about an ancestor who was a mail-order bride from Maine helped give Patricia MacLachlan the idea for the now famous character of Sarah from *Sarah, Plain and Tall.*

"When I drive along in my car, I have conversations with my characters. People think I'm singing along with the radio."

Allen Say   *pages 10–23*

Like Luke in *The Lost Lake,* Allen Say's daughter Yuriko spends part of her time living with her mother and part of her time with her father. Yuriko says that her earliest memories of her father are the wonderful stories he told her when she was very small. He made up the stories himself, and drew pictures to accompany his words as he spoke.

Books &

Author/Illustrator Study

More by Allen Say

Bicycle Man
This book is set in Japan shortly after World War II and is based on one of Allen Say's childhood memories.

El Chino
This biography uses beautiful pictures to help tell the story of a Chinese-American man who discovers his life's work on a visit to Spain.

Grandfather's Journey
This Caldecott-winning book tells the story of Allen Say's grandfather.

Allen Say

Fiction

Just My Luck
by Emily Moore
Olivia and Jeffrey set out to discover why Mrs. Dingle's poodle is missing.

To Find the Way
by Susan Nunes
illustrated by Cissy Greg
Long ago, the ancient Polynesians sailed from Tahiti to Hawaii. This book tells how a great navigator used his knowledge of astronomy to guide his people across thousands of miles of ocean.

Wingman
by Daniel Pinkwater
A boy who loves comic books invents his own Chinese-American superhero—Wingman. Together they fly over ancient China, and the boy learns to take pride in his heritage and its traditions.

Nonfiction

Discover Dinosaur Babies
by Miriam Schlein
Paleontologists describe their new discoveries about how dinosaur babies were cared for by their parents.

Night Dive
by Ann McGovern
photographs by Marin Scheiner and James Scheiner
A twelve-year-old girl describes the excitement of taking part in a scuba diving expedition at night.

One Giant Leap
by Mary Ann Fraser
Through art and text, the author recreates the drama of the first time humans walked on the moon.

xMedia

Videos

For All Mankind
Columbia Tristar
This documentary describes the Apollo mission to the moon, and how the astronauts prepared for the historical flight. (80 minutes)

Maricela
Public Media
Maricela and her mother have just come from El Salvador and are trying to adjust to life in the United States. With the help of some American friends, they discover many things about their homeland and about themselves. (55 minutes)

Sarah, Plain and Tall
Republic Home Video
This video, based on Patricia MacLachlan's beloved book, tells the story of how Anna and Caleb discover what it means to be a family. (98 minutes)

Software

Eagle Eye Mysteries: London
EA Kids
Join Jake and Jennifer Eagle in London as they solve 50 cases in historical locations.

Oceans Below
Software Toolworks (Macintosh, IBM, MPC)
Video clips, music, photos, and a dramatic narrative help make this almost as exciting as a real diving adventure.

Where in Space Is Carmen Sandiego?
Broderbund (Apple, Macintosh, IBM)
No longer content with stealing from folks on Earth, Carmen and her crew are loose in outer space! Track her across the universe in this exciting game.

Magazines

National Geographic World
National Geographic Society
This magazine has articles about outdoor adventure, new science discoveries, and unusual careers. The photographs create a you-are-there feeling.

Odyssey
Kalbach Publishing
This is the magazine to read if you want to keep up with the latest information on space exploration and astronomy.

A Place to Write

Kennedy Space Center,
Spaceport USA
Mail Code TWRS
Kennedy Space Center, FL 32899

Write for information about how the center operates, and what there is to see when you visit the center.

Acknowledgments

Grateful acknowledgment is made to the following sources for permission to reprint from previously published material. The publisher has made diligent efforts to trace the ownership of all copyrighted material in this volume and believes that all necessary permissions have been secured. If any errors or omissions have inadvertently been made, proper corrections will gladly be made in future editions.

Cover: © NASA.

Interior: "The Lost Lake" from THE LOST LAKE by Allen Say. Copyright © 1989 by Allen Say. Reprinted by permission of Houghton Mifflin Co. All rights reserved.

"Pushing the Limits" copyright © June 1992 by National Geographic Society. Reprinted with permission of *National Geographic WORLD. WORLD* is the official magazine for Junior Members of the National Geographic Society.

Text and book cover from SARAH, PLAIN AND TALL by Patricia MacLachlan. Text copyright © 1985 by Patricia MacLachlan. Cover illustration © 1987 by HarperCollins Publishers. Reprinted by permission of HarperCollins Publishers.

Selection from SCHOLASTIC ATLAS OF EXPLORATION by Dinah Starkey. Text and illustrations copyright © 1993 by HarperCollins Publishers Ltd. Used by permission.

"All the Way There" and cover from MATTHEW HENSON: ARCTIC EXPLORER by Sean Dolan, cover illustration by Bradford Brown. Copyright © 1992 by Chelsea House Publishers. Published by Chelsea House Publishers, a division of Main Line Book Co. Used by permission.

"Standing Up for Antarctica" reprinted by permission, *National Geographic WORLD.* Copyright © February 1991 by National Geographic Society.

"The Best New Thing" from THE BEST NEW THING by Isaac Asimov. Text copyright © 1971 by Isaac Asimov. Illustrations copyright © 1971 by the World Publishing Company. Reprinted by permission of HarperCollins Publishers.

Selection from U*S*KIDS, a *Weekly Reader* magazine, copyright © 1992 by Children's Better Health Institute, Benjamin Franklin Literary & Medical Society, Inc., Indianapolis, Indiana. Used by permission.

"The Great Kapok Tree" from THE GREAT KAPOK TREE: A TALE OF THE AMAZON RAIN FOREST by Lynne Cherry. Copyright © 1990 by Lynne Cherry. Reprinted by permission of Harcourt Brace & Company.

Selections and cover from THE DESERT BENEATH THE SEA by Ann McGovern and Eugenie Clark, illustrated by Craig Phillips. Text copyright © 1991 by Ann McGovern and Eugenie Clark. Illustrations copyright © 1991 by Craig Phillips. Reprinted by permission of Scholastic Inc.

Cover from DIGGING UP TYRANNOSAURUS REX by John R. Horner and Don Lessem. Illustration copyright © 1992 by Douglas Henderson. Photo credits: bottom photo Bruce Selyem/Museum of the Rockies; all others Greg Erickson/Museum of the Rockies. Published by Crown Publishers, Inc., a Random House Company.

Cover from JEM'S ISLAND by Kathryn Lasky, illustrated by Ronald Himler. Illustration copyright © 1982 by Ronald Himler. Published by Atheneum Books for Young Readers, Simon & Schuster Children's Publishing Division.

Cover from JUSTIN AND THE BEST BISCUITS IN THE WORLD by Mildred Pitts Walter, illustrated by Paul Tankersley. Illustration copyright © 1991 by Paul Tankersley. Published by Alfred A. Knopf, Inc.

Cover from WHO STOLE THE WIZARD OF OZ? by Avi, illustrated by Derek James. Cover illustration by Doron Ben-Ami. Cover art copyright © 1995 by Scholastic Inc. Originally published by Alfred A. Knopf, Inc.

Photography and Illustration Credits

Photos: © John Lei for Scholastic Inc., all Tool Box items unless otherwise noted. p. 2 cl: © Linda Drish for Scholastic Inc.; bl, tl: © John Bessler for Scholastic Inc.; p. 3 tc: © Telegraph Colour Library/FPG International Corp. pp. 2-3 background: NASA. p. 3 bc: NASA. p. 4 c: NASA/Peter Arnold, Inc.; tc: © Telegraph Colour Library/FPG International Corp. p. 5 c: © Ana Esperanza Nance for Scholastic Inc.; tc: © Telegraph Colour Library/FPG International Corp. p. 6 c: © David Jeffrey/The Image Bank; tc: © Telegraph Colour Library/FPG International Corp. pp. 8-9: © Team Russell/Adventure Photo & Film. pp. 24-29: © National Geographic Society. pp. 30-47: © Richard Megna/Fundamental Photographs. p. 48 tr: © Scala/Art Resource, NY; bl: © Barry Rosenthal/FPG International Corp.; br: © Sotheby Parke-Bernett/Art Resource, NY. p. 49 cr: © Sotheby Parke-Bernett/Art Resource, NY; tr: © J. Coolidge/The Image Bank. p. 50 br: © Stanley Bach for Scholastic Inc.; bc: © David Ball/The Stock Market; bl: © Travelpix/FPG International Corp. p. 51 bl: © W. & D. McIntyre/Photo Researchers, Inc.; br: NASA. pp. 52-53: © Al Grotell 1985. p. 54: © The Bettmann Archive. p. 56 tc: © Culver Pictures. pp. 58-59 tc: © The Bettmann Archive. p. 61 bc: © The Bettmann Archive; p. 63bc: © American Museum of Natural History. pp. 64-65 ghost back: © John Beatty/Tony Stone Worldwide. p.64 c: © The Cousteau Society; p. 65 br: © Peter Arnold Inc. br: © Peter Arnold Inc. p. 66 cl, tl, bl: © NASA; tr: NASA/JPL/TSADO/Tom Stack & Associates; tc: © Telegraph Colour Library/FPG International. p. 67 bl, c: NASA; br: © John Bessler for Scholastic Inc. p. 68: NASA. p. 69 c: © NASA/TSADO/Tom Stack & Associates; all others: NASA. pp. 84-85: © David Vaughn/Photo Researchers, Inc. p. 86 bl: © Stanley Bach for Scholastic Inc. p. 87 bl: © Stanley Bach for Scholastic Inc.; br: NASA. pp. 88-89: © J. Guichard/Sygma Scientific. pp. 116-117: © Todd Gipstein/Jason Foundation for Education. pp. 120-121 tc: © Todd Gipstein/Jason Foundation for Education; coral: © Herbert Schwartz/FPG International Corp. p. 122 br: © James Byron/The Stock Market. p. 123 bc: © Tony Freeman/Photo Edit; br: © John Lei for Scholastic Inc. p. 124 cr, bc: © John Lei for Scholastic Inc. p. 125 bl, bc, br: NASA; tr, cl: © Stanley Bach for Scholastic Inc. pp. 126-127 bc: © Stanley Bach for Scholastic Inc.; c: © John Lei for Scholastic Inc.; bc: © Tom Van Sant/Geosphere Project/The Stock Market; p. 127 tr: © WideWorld Photos Inc.; br: Courtesy NASA. p. 129 tc: NASA; bl: © Renee Lynn/Tony Stone Images. p. 131 tl: © Bud Lenhausen/Photo Researchers, Inc.; bl: © Tim Davis/Tony Stone Images. p. 132 cl: © Alex Gotfryd; bl: © Katie P. McManus; p. 133 br: © Richard Allen. p. 133 cr: © John MacLachlan. p. 133 tr: © Eugenie Clark. p. 134 br: © NASA/Peter Arnold, Inc. p. 135 br: © Stephen Ogilvy for Scholastic Inc.

Illustrations: pp. 48-49: Dinah Starkey; pp. 30, 33, 36, 40, 43, 47: Marni Backer; pp. 70-83: Tom Leonard.